P9-BZV-503

IS NOT JUST A NUMBER

THE ODYSSEY OF JACKIE ROBINSON, AMERICAN HERO

DOREEN RAPPAPORT

42 IS NOT JUST A NUMBER

CANDLEWICK PRESS

First edition 2017

Library of Congress Catalog Card Number pending
ISBN 978-0-7636-7624-7

17 18 19 20 21 22 BVG 10 9 8 7 6 5 4 3 2 1

Printed in Berryville, VA, U.S.A.

This book was typeset in Utopia.

Candlewick Press
99 Dover Street
Somerville, Massachusetts 02144

visit us at www.candlewick.com

Remembering Ira Landess,
sports fan supreme,
friend supreme

CONTENTS

1

THE NEIGHBORHOOD 1927

Eight-year-old Jack swept the last bit of dirt from the front steps into the dustpan. Mama was so proud of their five-bedroom house and wanted everything in it and around it to be neat and clean. The way his mother made good things happen, Jack liked to think of her as having magical powers.

Seven years earlier, when Jack's father abandoned the family, Mallie Robinson had packed up her five children and moved from Georgia to California with only three dollars sewn into the lining of her petticoat. Other members of Mallie's family came along, too: her sister, Cora Wade; Cora's husband, Sam; and their two sons.

Within only a few days of arriving in Pasadena, Mallie landed a job. For five days a week, fifty-two weeks a year, she cleaned and cooked for a white family. She worked hard for eight dollars a week, but she never complained. She was gone from early morning until night, so much of Jack's care fell to his older sister, Willa Mae.

For the first two years in California, the Robinsons and the Wades lived together in an apartment, sharing rent. Sam's job didn't pay much more than Mama's. Yet, miraculously, within two years, the families had squirreled away enough pennies and nickels and dimes for a down payment on a house.

When Mama saw 121 Pepper Street for sale, she thought it one of the finest on the block. The house, however, was in a white working-class neighborhood. The neighbors got an unpleasant surprise when the two black families moved into the two-story clapboard house. Someone burned a cross on the lawn. Another person went from house to house in the neighborhood to find someone who could buy them out, but no one had enough money. So the families stayed.

It took time, but Mama eventually won the respect of most of her white neighbors. She had sent Jack's older brother Edgar to do odd jobs at no charge for Mrs. Coppersmith, a widow who lived next door. A nearby bakery gave Mama its day-old leftovers. The milkman gave her unsold milk. Mallie could have easily used the baked goods and milk to help feed her large family, but she shared whatever she received with her neighbors, even the ones who were hostile.

Some neighbors still resented having a black family on the block. One frequently called the police to complain that Edgar, whizzing around on roller skates, made too much noise. An elderly couple scurried inside their house whenever any of the children walked their way.

Two years later, in 1924, Uncle Sam and Aunt Cora had saved enough money to buy a separate house, just a few blocks away. Now 121 Pepper Street belonged just to Mama, but she needed more money to meet expenses.

Jack wished he could help, but he was still too young to get paying jobs like his older brothers. Next year he might be able to get a newspaper route or mow lawns. For now, Mama believed that he could sweep, so he was going to do it, and do it good.

Mama's flowers were her pride and joy. So was the backyard, with its vegetable garden and fruit trees. Sometimes Mama raised turkeys, chickens, ducks, and rabbits, but her green thumb, livestock, and salary weren't always enough to feed her family of six. Many nights Jack's dinner was bread soaked in milk or in water and sugar, or leftovers that

Mama brought home from her job. Some mornings Jack was so hungry he could hardly stand up when he got to school.

Jack finished sweeping the front walk and moved on to the sidewalk. Across the street a girl was coming out of her house. She glared at Jack, then shouted, "Nigger, nigger, nigger."

As young and little as he was, Jack could not let this racial slur pass. His grandma Edna, born a slave, took great pride in being black and had taught Jack that Negro was the *only* proper name for their race. Any other name was a slur and should not be tolerated. In a flash, Jack was shouting, returning the insult with a cry of "cracker"— a derogatory term for poor rural whites in the South. The girl's father overheard Jack's taunt and charged outside to throw stones at Jack. Jack threw stones right back at him. Stones flew until the girl's mother came outside and yelled at her husband for fighting with a child.

2

JACK'S IDOL
1932

Jack idolized his older brother Mack, not just for his athletic ability but for his character and determination as well. In junior high school, Mack was already a star athlete in football, baseball, basketball, and track and field when he was diagnosed with a heart murmur. The school, fearing that something could happen to Mack if he played, banned him from all competitive sports. Mack refused to accept their decision and turned to his mother for help. Mallie met with school officials and convinced them to at least let Mack participate in non-contact sports. Mack returned to track and field and became a superstar sprinter. He won many events and set a statewide record for the high hurdles.

Mack was in high school now and hadn't lost a race so far this year. Today he was competing for John Muir Technical High School in the 100-yard dash. Jack tried never to miss watching a meet.

Jack was a natural athlete himself, always playing something. His keen hand-eye coordination made him a marbles champion. In games of dodgeball, Jack moved so fast that no one could ever hit him. With Jack on the field, his third-grade soccer team was so good that they were able to challenge the sixth-grade team and win. In the schoolyard at lunchtime, he played handball. No matter what game or sport, Jack always played to win, and usually did. For all the pride he took in his talents, however, he knew he could never run as fast as Mack.

Mack crouched in starting position: hips up, weight resting on his fingertips. A sprinter had to be ready to run as soon as the pistol signaled the start of the race, so his stance was critical. So was reaction time. There wasn't a split second to lose.

The pistol shot popped. Jack watched Mack take off, spraying dirt behind him. Mack pumped his legs hard, his eyes focused on the track. He never looked over his shoulder or to the side. That could add fractions of a second to his time and cost him the race.

Jack knew that Mack was thinking of only one thing: winning.

Mack picked up speed, and Jack yelled and cheered along with every other Muir fan as his brother crossed the finish line ahead of the pack.

3

"INTERNATIONAL DAY"
SUMMER 1934

Jack undressed quickly and put on his bathing suit. He and his "gang" were going to have a chance to cool off today at Pasadena's municipal pool. The Pepper Street Gang, as they called themselves, was a mix of poor black, Mexican, Japanese, and a few white kids. They didn't carry knives or guns or take drugs or drink alcohol. They didn't even have a clubhouse or jackets or a secret handshake. Restricted from activities in the city because of race and money, they had banded together to create their own fun. Jack intended to have lots of fun at the pool this day.

The Pepper Street Gang's fun wasn't always legal. They stole fruit from produce stands. They hid out on the local golf course, scooped up balls that came by, and then sold them back to the players. They threw rocks and dirt at passing cars. Once they spread tar on the lawn of a man who had shouted racist slurs at them. When Mallie found out about that, she made the boys clean up the mess. Many times Jack had been hauled down to police headquarters for a lecture by the head of the police Youth Division. Once he had been arrested for swimming in the city reservoir during a heat wave. Today's fun would be completely legal, though it would definitely annoy the white lifeguard.

Summer temperatures in Pasadena hovered around ninety degrees Fahrenheit. On most sweltering days, Jack and his friends could only peek through the picket fence around Pasadena's municipal pool and watch the white kids swim. But today was Wednesday, what city officials called "International Day." It was the one day a week when, for three hours, blacks, Latinos, and Asians were allowed to swim at the municipal pool. After those three hours were up, the pool would be drained, cleaned, and refilled with fresh water, all before the next morning, when Pasadena's white citizens would return to swim.

The municipal pool was only one of numerous humiliations that blacks faced in Pasadena. There were no "White Only" signs as there were in the South, but race segregation was still the rule. Jack could get a job washing dishes at Schrafft's restaurant, but he wouldn't be allowed to eat at the counter. There were neighborhoods he knew he wouldn't be safe in. He yearned to use the sports equipment at the YMCA, but membership wasn't open to blacks. Whenever he could, Jack defied segregation. A few times Jack and a friend sat down at a Woolworth's lunch counter and refused to budge until they were served. More than once, when the lights dimmed in a movie theater, he snuck into the white section.

Mama had moved the family to Pasadena because her half brother, who had settled in California, had told her that if she wanted "to get closer to heaven," she should visit California. Jack believed that was true, but only if you were white and wealthy.

Bigotry was ingrained in Pasadena's schools, yet Jack formed warm bonds with his kindergarten and first-grade teachers. As the years passed, however, other white teachers revealed their prejudices: they were often rude and excluded minority students from activities. More than once, Jack and his friends got blamed for trouble that was actually caused by white students.

Mama believed education was the one thing white people couldn't take away from a person. That might be true, Jack thought, but no matter how well educated he could become, he knew that the city of Pasadena would never hire him as a police officer or a firefighter or a teacher or a janitor. He and his friends would be lucky if they got jobs picking up garbage.

With the afternoon sun beating down on him, Jack climbed the ladder to the highest diving platform. He looked down at the kids swimming and those scattered around the edges of the concrete pool. Then he looked across at the white lifeguard sitting in his high chair, watching Jack, waiting for him to dive. The lifeguard was in for a surprise.

Up and out Jack jumped, as high as he could. He grabbed and hugged his legs close to his chest. He dropped through the air like a bomb, hitting the water with an explosive splash and drenching everyone in and around the pool with his cannonball. Even before Jack surfaced, he knew that the lifeguard was already climbing down from his chair to warn Jack against repeating that stunt.

But Wednesday was Jack's day. He was going to cannonball as often as he liked, no matter what the lifeguard said. No one was going to stop him.

4

MACK'S BIG CHALLENGE
JULY 18, 1936

It was 3:00 a.m., but no one in the Robinson family was sleeping. The 1936 Olympic Games in Berlin, Germany, were under way, and, like millions of other Americans, they were huddled around the radio. This year's Olympics were particularly personal for Jack and his family. The American track and field team had two black women and sixteen black men on it, three times the number of African Americans who had competed in the previous Olympics. Twenty-two-year-old Mack Robinson was one of them.

Nazi dictator Adolf Hitler had built a gigantic stadium in Berlin, confident that German athletes would outshine all others and prove the rightness of his theory that Aryans were the master race.

The Olympics were a chance for African-American athletes, banned from all professional sports except boxing in their own country, to show the United States and the world what they could do. And over the years, when given the chance, black athletes had proved that they were as talented as white athletes.

In 1904, George Poage, the first black American on a U.S. Olympic team, won bronze medals in the 200-meter and 400-meter hurdles. Four years later, John Baxter Taylor won a gold in the 4x400 relay. The 1924 Olympics saw three black American medalists. In the long jump, DeHart Hubbard won the gold and Ed Gourdin won the silver. Earle Johnson won the bronze for the 10,000-meter cross-country race.

In 1932, black sprinter Eddie Tolan (the "Midnight Express") had awed spectators by capturing the gold in both the 100- and 200-meter races. Ralph Metcalfe had won a silver in the 100-meter and a bronze in the 200-meter.

At Pasadena Junior College, Mack had set national records in the 100-meter, the 200-meter, and the long jump, yet his exceptional achievements had not paved an easy road to Berlin.

The United States was still struggling through an economic depression; money was even scarcer for black Americans than it was for white Americans. Most white Olympic athletes had college coaches who trained them in the nuances of their sport and the styles of the other competitors so they would know what they were up against. Their colleges paid for all equipment, travel, and living expenses. Even in the best of economic times, few African-American athletes ever enjoyed such backing. Pasadena Junior College didn't have the money to help Mack. Mack hadn't even had the $150 train fare to get from California to New York City for the qualifying trials. Lucky for him, some Pasadena businesspeople got together and donated the train fare, but they hadn't given him money for new running shoes. Mack was still stuck running in battered spikes that pinched his toes.

The announcer called the names of the runners in the 200-meter dash. Among them was American Jesse Owens, who would be Mack's fiercest competitor. Owens's extraordinary accomplishments were well known. In high school, he matched a world record in the 100-yard dash. At the 1935 NCAA championships, he won the 100-yard dash, tying the world mark. Ten minutes later, he broke the world record in the long jump. Nine minutes after that, he set another world record, in the 220-yard dash. And several minutes later, he broke another world record, in the low hurdles. He won the same four events at the Big Ten Track and Field Championships in Michigan the following May. He was fast, but so was Mack.

The pistol sounded, and the runners were off. Before

Jack knew it, the announcer was booming the names of the winners: Jesse Owens, first, with a gold medal. His time: 20.7 seconds. Behind Owens by four-tenths of a second, Mack Robinson had captured the silver.

There was no end to the joy and pride in the Robinson home that morning.

Out of a total of fifty-six medals won by the United States in the 1936 Olympics, fourteen were won in track and field. Black athletes won all fourteen. Eight of the fourteen medals were gold.

Mack and his teammates had a triumphant post-Olympic tour in Europe, competing in many events. In Paris, Mack tied the world record in a 200-meter race.

But when the Olympic silver medalist returned home to Pasadena, there were no ticker-tape parades. The city ignored Mack's accomplishment. The Olympics behind him, the star athlete needed a job, and found himself sweeping the streets of Pasadena on the night shift.

5

A NEW PATH
JANUARY 1938

Jack and his friends were hanging out at the corner of Morton and Mountain Streets when a car pulled up beside them. A man leaned out the open window. "Is Jack Robinson here?" he asked. Jack didn't answer, and his friends didn't give him away either.

"Tell him I want to see him at the junior church," the man said, and drove away.

Karl Everette Downs was the new minister at the United Methodist church that Jack's mother attended. Mallie's faith in God as a source of strength and comfort was unshakable. Jack went to church because Mallie made him go.

One of the minister's biggest goals and challenges was

to persuade young people to come back into the church. He wanted to help them understand that Jesus's message was relevant to them, to show them that they could gather strength and hope from it. Downs was determined to make his church a welcoming place for young people, but first he had to get them there.

Downs was well aware of Jack's athletic feats. There was no sport the nineteen-year-old did not excel in, making him a hero to many minority youths in Pasadena. Jack had been the leading scorer, rebounder, and passer on Muir's high-school basketball team. His fielding as shortstop and his baserunning had brought many a victory to the high-school baseball team. His dazzling speed and throwing arm had catapulted the Muir football team to eleven wins and gotten them close to the league championship. Though he rarely played tennis, Jack had even won the junior boys' singles championship in the Pacific Coast Negro Tennis Tournament. He was continuing to pile up triumphs at Pasadena Junior College.

Jack Robinson was just the kind of young man who could help lead other young men back to church. If Downs could win over Jack, he could win over others, too. He also knew that Jack had been arrested a couple of times. The first had been for swimming in the city reservoir. Then, only a few weeks earlier, Jack and a friend had been arrested after leaving a movie theater. They were singing a popular song of the day. A police officer within earshot objected to the lyrics of the song. An exchange between the three men landed Jack in jail for a night and got him an additional sentence of ten days. The judge suspended the sentence and put him on probation.

When Jack eventually went to see Downs, he found the minister different from any other man of God he'd known. For one thing, the Reverend Karl Downs was young, only seven years older than Jack. He was fun and easy to talk to. Downs had played basketball and softball, and pretty well at that. Growing up in Texas, he had faced the "White Only" signs every day yet refused to let segregation defeat him.

Most important, the minister knew how to listen, and he seemed to understand the way Jack felt about many things. Jack talked about his pain and concern over how hard his mother still worked to support the family. She was always giving to other people when she should have been taking care of herself. He so wanted to ease her financial burden, but as a college student working part-time, he earned only enough for his expenses. Jack knew how much Mallie valued education, but he felt uncertain about staying in college.

The Reverend Karl Downs did not solve Jack's problems, but his warmth and concern helped Jack cope with his difficult feelings. The teachings of the church became central to Jack's life. He began to understand the power of faith. He began to believe what his mother believed: that faith in God would help him navigate his way through life. Before going to sleep every night, Jack kneeled at the side of his bed and said his prayers.

As Downs had hoped, Jack brought his friends to the church, and it became a center of social and athletic activities. There were dances and badminton and basketball games. Jack's tie to the Reverend Karl Downs became stronger and stronger. No matter how tired he was from playing football on Saturday, Jack got up early every Sunday to teach the younger children in Sunday school.

6

UNIVERSITY LIFE
FEBRUARY 1939–MARCH 1941

Local reporters, writing about Jack's remarkable athletic exploits at Pasadena Junior College, had given him the nickname Jackie, and it stuck with fans and friends. His two years at junior college had come to an end, and he was ready to transfer to a four-year college. Jackie knew that if he were white, he would have been swamped by athletic scholarship offers. USC (the University of Southern California) did offer him a football scholarship, but it was well known that its coach was prejudiced, and Jackie would likely end up on the bench for most of the football season.

The University of Oregon, where Mack studied on an athletic scholarship, reached out to him, but Jackie didn't want to go that far from home.

His brother Frank, Jackie's greatest fan, encouraged him to go to UCLA (the University of California at Los Angeles). Tuition was free, and the sports department welcomed talented black athletes. Halfback Kenny Washington and receiver Woody Strode were already football stars there. And if Jackie played football, he wouldn't have to spend money for lunch. Athletes ate for free at UCLA's training table.

So on February 15, 1939, Jackie drove his rickety old Plymouth the twenty-five miles to UCLA to start his junior year as a commuter. Like Pasadena Junior College, UCLA was not officially race segregated, but Jackie and the forty-nine other black students knew their place on this campus of 9,600. It went without saying that they would socialize only among themselves; they would not be invited to campus parties. They would never have a black professor or instructor. Even if Jackie had had the money to live near campus, he couldn't: African Americans were restricted from living in the neighborhoods around the university.

Though his tuition was free, Jackie still needed a job to earn money for gas and incidental expenses. The only jobs the university offered black male students were janitorial, so Jackie took one. Unexpectedly, two owners of an off-campus bookstore, who did not share the university's prejudices, gave him a second job.

UCLA's coaches were disappointed when Jackie announced that he would not play any sports in his first term in order to focus on his studies. But when the next term came, he tried out for football and made the team.

Fans thronged to see Jackie Robinson, Kenny Washington, and Woody Strode lead UCLA to six wins and four ties for an undefeated season. Jackie dazzled fans with his speed and baffled his opponents with his sudden moves and fakes.

When football season was over, Jackie turned to basketball. Fans cheered as he twisted and turned, dribbling the ball down the court. He shot well from anywhere, rarely missing the hoop.

In the spring, Jackie ran track and won the long-jump title at the NCAA nationals, setting a new record. As if track and field weren't enough for one season, he also played baseball. His speed and concentration on the diamond, his flawless fielding, and his signature base-stealing set him apart from all other players. Jackie became the first UCLA student ever to earn letters in four sports in a single year.

Love entered Jackie Robinson's life in his second year at UCLA. He had seen seventeen-year-old Rachel Annetta

Isum around campus and at Kerckhoff Hall, where black students gathered between classes. He had felt too shy to speak to her, so his friend Ray Bartlett introduced them. Rachel already knew Jackie as a local football star. She had seen him play at Pasadena Junior College and thought him conceited, but his smile and confidence warmed her to him now, and they began dating.

Rachel told Jackie of her dream to be a nurse. She shared her dream of having a family. Jackie told Rachel of wanting to be a coach for young people and his dream of having a family. Mallie Robinson believed that Rachel was the perfect partner for her son: churchgoing, nondrinking, nonsmoking, and a straight-A student.

Three months before Jackie was due to graduate, he decided to leave college. His brother Frank had died in a motorcycle accident two years earlier, and Frank's widow and two children were now living in the Robinson home on Pepper Street, along with Willa Mae, Edgar, Mack, and Mack's wife. Jackie's mother had also taken in a nephew whose mother had died, and had just bought a second house on Pepper Street.

For twenty-two years, Jackie's mother had bent over people's beds, sinks, and toilets, cleaning up their messes. Before that, she had bent over crops in the fields. It was time for her to be taken care of, time for her to stop giving so much to everyone else in the family. Jackie decided he would get a full-time job to help his mother and to save enough money to marry Rachel. He would coach kids. Maybe he could supplement his income and satisfy his love of sports by playing semiprofessional football.

Everyone close to him—the Reverend Karl Downs, his coaches, his mother, and Rachel—tried to convince him not to leave school. UCLA offered him extra financial support if he would stay on, but he wouldn't be talked out of leaving. He had garnered awards for his brilliant athletic achievements but had no future in professional sports. No black athlete did. He saw no point in being in school any longer.

The United States was still in an economic depression. To help unemployed Americans, the government had created public works jobs, and millions of Americans were constructing public buildings, roads, parks, and schools. Jackie got a job with the National Youth Administration as an assistant athletic director at a job-training camp in Atascadero, California, but within three months, the government ended the program. Jackie then managed to get a day job working construction at the U.S. naval base at Pearl Harbor, Oahu, Hawaii. His night job was playing for a semiprofessional football team there.

It felt good to be sending money to his mother, but the construction job didn't last long. Neither did playing semiprofessional football. An old football injury in his right ankle flared up, and he played poorly. Homesick and disappointed, he left Pearl Harbor on December 5, 1941.

Two days later, in a surprise attack, the Japanese bombed the naval base at Pearl Harbor, pulling the United States into the Second World War. On March 23, 1942, Jackie received notice that he had been drafted into the army.

7

FROM PRIVATE TO LIEUTENANT
JULY–AUGUST 1942

In nine weeks of basic training at Fort Riley, Kansas, the constant push-ups, sit-ups, mile runs, climbing rope bridges and ladders, and rappelling down fifty-foot wooden walls had tested every bit of Jackie's strength and endurance. His football injury plagued him through it all, but he had passed with flying colors. He was ranked an "expert" marksman, and his character was rated "excellent." Along with other black soldiers in his unit, he applied to Officer Candidate School (OCS).

Three months passed. He should have been accepted into OCS by now. So should the other black soldiers in his unit who had passed basic training with flying colors. White privates who had performed less well had been accepted. Yet here he was, stuck grooming horses. He was outraged.

Segregation and prejudice existed in the army as in civilian life. Blacks and whites were separated into different units, slept in separate barracks, and ate in separate mess halls. Even the buses on the base were segregated. When Jackie tried to join Fort Riley's baseball team, a white player told him that the officer in charge had said, "I'll break up the team before I'll have a nigger on it."

Frustrated and determined, Jackie, along with a group of other black soldiers, went seeking an answer: If they had passed all the tests for OCS, why were *they* not in school? Their question came to naught. Jackie knew that the army didn't consider Negroes "officer material."

He shared his frustration with his friend Joe Louis, another recruit at the base, who happened to be the heavyweight boxing champion of the world. In his career, Louis had won twenty-seven fights in a row. Then, on June 19, 1936, a German boxer named Max Schmeling beat him. Joe didn't let that defeat keep him down. He kept fighting to get his crown back, and he did. Even then, he wasn't satisfied. "I don't want nobody to call me champ until I beat Schmeling," he had announced to the world. In a rematch, Louis knocked out Schmeling in just two minutes and four seconds in the first round. American pride soared.

Joe Louis knew lots of important people and, after listening to Jackie's plight, telephoned a friend who worked for the secretary of war. That call prompted an investigation, and in early November, Jackie and a small group of other black soldiers were finally admitted into OCS. It was a first in the army, a barrier broken: black and white soldiers working, studying, eating, and living together.

On January 28, 1943, Jackie received his gold bars, becoming a second lieutenant in the cavalry of the U.S. Army. His leadership ability and his character earned him the appointment of morale officer of his unit. None of his achievements, however, gained him admittance into the white officers' club, nor did they end discriminatory promotion practices: he would never be promoted over a white officer in his unit. It was even questionable whether any black soldiers would ever be sent into combat; most were being placed into service units.

There was nothing Jackie could do to change those policies, but when some black soldiers complained bitterly about their treatment at the PX (the post exchange, or on-base store), he decided to see what he could do about it. All soldiers shopped at the PX. It was like a department store where soldiers could buy food, clothing, and sundries. It was often crowded, and it could take time until shoppers were able to make their purchases. Seating was segregated, and there were far fewer chairs available in the black section than in the white section. When those limited seats filled up, black soldiers often found themselves standing, even if seats designated for whites were empty.

Jackie decided to confront the matter head-on. From company headquarters, he telephoned the provost marshal, head of the military police on the base. Jackie did not challenge the segregated policy. He merely asked that more seats be provided for black soldiers. This lack of adequate accommodations was an indignity for his fellow soldiers, he protested. The provost's response made it clear that he did not care about the dignity of black soldiers. Jackie continued to press his point anyway.

The provost, who did not know Jackie and so was unaware that he was black, finally excused the lack of seating by saying, "Lieutenant, let me put it to you this way. How would you like to have your wife sitting next to a nigger?"

Unable to contain his anger, Jackie shouted back, asking the provost if he knew how close his wife had ever been to a nigger.

Jackie's outburst caused all work and conversation around him to stop. Silence fell over company headquarters. No one could believe what he had just said to a superior officer. Jackie ranted on. The provost, who couldn't get a word in, finally hung up.

Jackie's protest got results, however: more seats were added to the PX area reserved for black soldiers.

On April 13, three months after receiving their second lieutenant bars, Jackie and other black officers at Fort Riley were notified that they were being sent to Camp Hood, Texas, to join the 761st Tank Battalion and prepare to fight in Europe.

8

THE CONFRONTATION
JULY 6–NOVEMBER 28, 1944

Jackie stood waiting for the army bus to take him on the first leg of his trip to the military hospital in Temple, Texas. It was eleven p.m. and hot and muggy. Day or night, summer in Fort Hood, Texas, was unbearable, with temperatures regularly reaching into the hundreds. Jackie's battalion—the 761st—was shipping out for Europe in two weeks. His commanding officer wanted Jackie to go as the battalion's morale officer, but Jackie's old ankle injury still gave him trouble. In the morning, doctors would examine Jackie and make the final decision as to whether he was fit for combat.

The bus pulled up. Jackie got on. Walking down the

aisle, he saw Virginia Jones, the wife of another black officer, sitting in the middle of the bus. He sat down beside her and settled in for some friendly conversation. A few blocks later, the civilian driver, Milton Renegar, stopped the bus, walked back to Jackie, and ordered him to move to the rear. Jackie realized that Renegar must have seen him and Virginia Jones through his rearview mirror and assumed, because Virginia was light skinned, that Jackie was sitting next to and talking to a white woman. Such behavior by a black man was totally unacceptable in the South. Jackie refused Renegar's order.

Public buses in Texas cities and towns were still segregated, but Jackie was on an army bus on an army base. Just one month earlier, the army had outlawed segregation on all vehicles on military bases. There was no reason for Jackie to move to the back of the bus, so he didn't.

The bus rolled on. When Renegar realized that Jackie had not moved, he stopped the bus again, returned to Jackie, and shouted at him to move. Jackie didn't budge. Renegar threatened that he would make trouble for Jackie if he didn't. Still Jackie refused. Their verbal duel became even more heated; neither man was going to yield.

When the bus pulled up to the last stop on the army base, a passenger, a white woman who worked in the Fort Hood kitchen, declared that she was going to press charges against Jackie.

"That's all right," Jackie said. "I don't care."

Renegar asked Jackie to show him some identification. Jackie refused to do that, too. When Jackie overheard Renegar tell people at the bus stop, "This nigger is making trouble," Jackie marched over, put his finger right in Renegar's face, and cursed him. Someone called the military police.

When the military police arrived, they correctly addressed Jackie, an officer, as "sir" and respectfully asked him to accompany them to tell their commander what had happened. Virginia Jones offered to go with Jackie to corroborate his story, but Jackie told her it wasn't necessary. He was confident that when he explained what had transpired, it would be clear that he was in the right. He had broken no rules.

But Captain Gerald M. Bear, the commander of the military police, didn't seem interested in hearing what Jackie had to say. Bear ordered him into an anteroom to wait while he questioned two white guardhouse officers about what had happened. Jackie couldn't believe it. Those guards hadn't even been on the bus. Anything they might have known about the incident they learned secondhand. Bear wasn't treating him with the respect due an officer. Jackie wasn't going to allow this. He followed Bear into his office, protesting that he should be questioned instead.

"Nobody comes into the room until I tell him," Bear warned.

When Bear finally called Jackie into his office, two white women were already there. The one with the pad was obviously a stenographer, but who was the other woman who immediately started firing questions at him? And where did she get the authority to do so? She threw her questions out so fast, he didn't even have time to respond. When he told her to stop interrupting him, she stomped out of the room.

Captain Bear growled that Jackie was "an uppity nigger" and "had no right to speak to that lady in that manner."

"I feel I have as much right to tell my story as she has to ask questions," Jackie countered.

The captain fumed. In the end, he brought Jackie up on two charges: behaving with disrespect toward a superior officer, and willfully disobeying a lawful command to remain in an anteroom until summoned.

These charges were serious. Jackie was facing a court-martial. If found guilty, he could lose his rank as an officer, be dishonorably discharged from the army, or be imprisoned. A conviction would follow him for the rest of his life. It was hard enough being black without such a stain on his record. Yet Jackie wasn't afraid. He had done nothing wrong and had every intention of testifying to that. He believed, as his mother did, that God would take care of him.

At the trial, Jackie's lawyer pointed out inconsistencies between statements made by Captain Bear and the two guardhouse officers. Jackie's commanding officer testified to his outstanding character and skills. Other soldiers in Jackie's battalion testified to his integrity and reputation.

Though not required to, Jackie chose to take the stand. He admitted that he had used obscene language with the bus driver but not with a woman. He further explained that being referred to as a "nigger" by the driver had particularly provoked him: his maternal grandmother, a former slave, had taught him that "nigger" was an unacceptable and contemptuous term. "I am a Negro," he asserted, "not a nigger." He insisted that Bear had not treated him with the respect due an officer.

In his summation to the jury, Jackie's lawyer stated that this was "simply a situation in which a few individuals sought to vent their bigotry on a Negro they considered 'uppity' because he had the audacity . . . to exercise rights that belonged to him as an American and as a soldier."

Jackie was acquitted on both charges.

By the time the trial was over, Jackie's battalion had already left for Europe. He was reassigned to another battalion, but he asked to serve instead in the Special Service Division in the area of recreation. He was told there were no openings for "colored" officers there. He appealed to remain on active duty in a limited-service status, perhaps working in a defense plant, where he could be useful to the war effort. That request was denied, too, and he was assigned to yet another battalion. He appealed again, explaining that he wasn't fit for infantry service because of his old football injury.

On November 28, 1944, Jackie was transferred to Camp Breckinridge, in Kentucky, where he was "honorably relieved from active duty . . . by reason of physical disqualification." He was twenty-six years old, with no prospects for a job.

Shortly after that, Jackie by chance ran into Ted Alexander, who, before he was drafted into the army, had played for the Kansas City Monarchs in the Negro American League. The Negro leagues had developed to counter the exclusion of black athletes from Major League Baseball. They played two hundred games a year and brought pride to the thousands of black Americans who attended their games. Alexander told him that the Monarchs needed players because so much of the team had been drafted into the armed services. For Jackie, who despised segregation and had fought it as best he could since he was little, the leagues were a poor second, but it was a job. And he would be doing what he loved. He wrote to the Monarchs' manager and was accepted on a tryout basis to spring training.

9

IN THE NEGRO LEAGUES MARCH–AUGUST 1945

Jackie closed his eyes and shifted his body about, trying to find a comfortable position on the bus seat. He wanted to block out the banter of the other ballplayers. It wasn't that their talk wasn't valuable to him. As a first-year shortstop, Jackie had learned a great deal from these outstanding athletes, on and off the field. Win or lose, after each game his teammates chewed over the details—the hits, misses, steals, strikeouts.

After they played the Homestead Grays, there was always talk of James "Cool Papa" Bell. People said Bell was faster than Hall-of-Famer Ty Cobb. It was a common joke that Bell moved so fast, you couldn't see his feet touch the ground. Jackie thought *he* was fast, but would he ever equal Bell? It seemed impossible.

And what a joy to be on the same team as the great pitcher Satchel Paige. No doubt he had the fastest arm in the world. And, oh, how Satchel made everyone laugh, swearing that his "bee ball" was so fast, a batter only heard it buzz as it zinged past him.

But right now, Jackie didn't want to listen or learn. He needed sleep. The playing schedule was grueling. The Monarchs had played a doubleheader that ended late that night, and now they were on the move again. Day after day, they'd finish a game or two, get back on the bus, and travel long distances to another town and another ballpark. Sometimes Jackie was so tired, he played while half asleep.

Bus travel was bad, but the sleeping accommodations were worse. In the South and Midwest, hotels were segregated. The team always ended up in cheap, dingy lodgings. Sometimes the rooms were so dirty that Jackie opted to sleep on the bus instead. Finding places to eat was equally difficult. They were lucky if they found a restaurant that would even let them order takeout. Even then, they couldn't go through the front door to order it or pick it up. They had to slip in through the back so the white customers wouldn't see them. Sometimes they just bought the makings of sandwiches in a grocery store and fixed their own. Meals were eaten on the moving bus, not great for digestion. In some towns, the team was permitted only on the baseball field and was banned from using the lockers or showers. And the "White" and "Colored" signs everywhere infuriated them.

Jackie was grateful to have a job, and grateful that black athletes had this opportunity to show the world their talent, but he could not stand the constant humiliations.

The bus pulled into a gas station in a small town to fill up. Jackie asked the attendant where the bathrooms were.

"Yours is over there," said the attendant, gesturing vaguely.

"What do you mean my bathroom? There's a bathroom right here," Jackie said, walking toward the closest bathroom, which was marked "White." The attendant rushed at Jackie, yelling and cursing at him for daring to defy segregation. Jackie's anger won out, and he hit the attendant in the head. Jackie's teammates ran over and pulled him away. The team's traveling secretary slapped the gas money on the pump, and their bus took off.

His teammates warned him against ever doing that again: if there had been other white people at the station, they might not have gotten away alive.

He knew his teammates were right. He had put them all in danger. He couldn't continue with this life much longer. Maybe the majors would integrate eventually, but not in his lifetime.

Rachel had graduated from UCLA in June as the most outstanding clinical nurse in her class. They wanted to marry soon. When the season ended, he would follow the Reverend Karl Downs's advice and get a job as a high-school coach. It wouldn't be like playing Major League Baseball, but he thought he would like working with young people.

10

ADVOCATES FOR CHANGE 1937–1947

As a young pitcher, Wendell Smith had suffered the pain of being shut out of Major League Baseball. He had been brought to tears when a baseball scout told him that in spite of his talent, his color banned him from the majors. Now a sportswriter for the *Pittsburgh Courier,* the most important black weekly in the country, Smith channeled his disappointment and anger into words and direct action. While other black activists pressed for equality for their people in other fields, Smith had committed his life to integrating Major League Baseball.

In his columns, Smith countered the many arguments about why integration wouldn't work: black athletes weren't good enough; they didn't want to play in the majors anyway; white ballplayers would never accept them as teammates; and white fans would never come to see them play, destroying the business of baseball. Smith reminded readers of the extraordinary talent and popularity of boxer Joe Louis and runner Jesse Owens.

He interviewed National League managers to see how they felt about hiring black athletes and found only one opposed. All, however, declared that the decision was not theirs to make—it was the owners'.

Other black sportswriters led their own crusades. Frank Young of the *Chicago Defender,* Sam Lacy of the *Baltimore Afro-American,* and Joe Bostic of the Harlem *People's Voice* decried racial segregation and emphasized the outsize talents of many Negro league players. White journalists Ed Sullivan and Shirley Povich pointed out the great injustice that black Americans, fighting and dying in World War II to protect Europe's freedom, were second-class citizens at home. Labor union members in New York City stood outside Yankee Stadium, Ebbets Field, and the Polo Grounds and collected more than a million signatures on petitions to end segregated baseball.

The most active group pressing the issue was the American Communist Party. Reporters Lester Rodney and Bill Mardo of the communist weekly the *Daily Worker* were unrelenting in criticizing segregation in America's pastime. The newspaper organized parades, and thousands of New Yorkers marched, carrying signs calling for an end to Jim Crow in baseball. In the summer of 1943, Wendell Smith and Nat Low, sports editor of the *Daily Worker,* managed to pressure the Pittsburgh Pirates to hold tryouts for two black ballplayers, but the invitation was withdrawn. On opening day in 1945, members of the Communist Party picketed Yankee Stadium. One of their many banners read "If We Can Stop Bullets, Why Not Balls?"

In 1942, Commissioner of Baseball Kenesaw M. Landis denied the color barrier: "There is no rule, formal or informal, or any understanding—unwritten, subterranean, or sub-anything—against the hiring of Negro players by the teams of organized ball." Landis's denials, however, didn't fool any activists: his anti-integration stand was well known.

In November 1944, Landis died suddenly. Three months later, New York State legislators passed the Ives-Quinn law, forbidding discrimination in hiring on the basis of race, creed, or color. New York City's mayor, Fiorello La Guardia, seized the opportunity and asked sportswriter Sam Lacy, manager Larry MacPhail of the New York Yankees, manager Branch Rickey of the Brooklyn Dodgers, and Joseph H. Rainey, a black judge from Philadelphia, to serve on a committee to examine discrimination in the major leagues. Unfortunately the group never met; MacPhail always had an excuse for why he couldn't attend meetings.

In April, Boston city councillor Isadore Muchnick, who had been pressuring his two home teams to integrate, finally succeeded in getting the Red Sox to agree to tryouts for black athletes. Wendell Smith brought Jackie and two other Negro league players, Sam Jethroe and Marvin Williams. Their performances were stellar, but the Red Sox didn't even give them the courtesy of a letter of rejection. Jackie was disgusted: he had traveled fifteen hundred miles for nothing. Smith later learned that the Sox's chief scout had said about Jackie, "What a ballplayer! Too bad he's the wrong color."

That same month, A. B. "Happy" Chandler, a former United States senator and governor of Kentucky, was appointed to replace Landis as baseball commissioner. Black reporters noted that as governor, Chandler had perpetuated segregated education by building separate schools for black children. In an interview, however, Chandler declared, "I don't believe in barring Negroes from baseball just because they are Negroes." Civil rights activists wondered if he had had a change of heart, if he might become an ally in the struggle.

On April 6, sportswriter Joe Bostic, ever persistent for the cause, arrived unannounced at the Dodger training camp at Bear Mountain, New York, with two Negro league players and demanded tryouts for them. Though incensed, Branch Rickey agreed, but he chastised Bostic. "I'm more for your cause than anybody else you know," he said, "but you are making a mistake using force. You are defeating your own aims." Rickey held a press conference shortly after the tryouts, where he attacked the Negro leagues as "rackets" and declared that he was going to create a new Negro team.

Black columnist Ludlow W. Werner summed up the feelings of most integration advocates: "It would be a hot day in December before Rickey would ever have a Negro wear the uniform of organized [white] baseball."

11

THE INTERVIEW
AUGUST 28, 1945

It was a humid August day when Jackie climbed the stairs of 215 Montague Street in Brooklyn. Dodger scout Clyde Sukeforth had seen Jackie play with the Monarchs and told him that Branch Rickey wanted to meet him. Rickey was interested in creating a new "colored" team, which he would call the Brooklyn Brown Dodgers. Sukeforth said that if Jackie couldn't come to Rickey, Rickey would come to Jackie. Jackie was intrigued and decided to go to Brooklyn to meet Rickey.

Branch Rickey was a baseball wonder and innovator. He had created the farm club system, where young ball-players got training and time to prove themselves worthy of advancing to the majors. In his twenty-five years with the St. Louis Cardinals, he had developed talent that led the team to three pennants and three World Series victories. None of that talent was black.

Though politically conservative, Rickey was a deeply religious man and believed that segregation was a profound moral injustice. At twenty-three, as coach of the Ohio Wesleyan University baseball team, he had seen firsthand how segregation damaged a person. Once when he was on the road with his team, a hotel refused lodgings to the team's only black player. Rickey protested to the hotel manager, and finally the player, Charles Thomas, was allowed to sleep on a cot in Rickey's room. The acute emotional pain and humiliation that Thomas suffered that night still haunted Rickey. Yet never before in his entire career had he demonstrated any interest in integrating the major leagues. In spite of his silence all those years, Rickey did believe that talented black athletes deserved the same opportunities as white athletes.

Now Rickey was in New York, one of the country's most liberal cities, in the state that had just passed the Ives-Quinn Act, forbidding discrimination in hiring. Fiorello La Guardia, New York City's mayor, wanted the three New York baseball teams to uphold that law and integrate their teams. It seemed the right time and place to challenge baseball's unwritten color ban. Rickey's moral commitment to integrating the majors was nevertheless entwined with his competitive nature, a sharp business sense, and the thought that if he succeeded, he would secure a place for himself in the history books.

Rickey wanted the Dodgers to triumph as his Cardinals had, but the present team was weak and needed new blood. That meant finding talent, of which there was plenty in the Negro leagues. The right black athlete could help revitalize the Dodgers and help them win the pennant. Integration might temporarily alienate old fans, but it would bring new fans—many of them black—and more money into the Dodger coffers. Rickey also knew it would bring much trouble for the black athlete he chose to break the color barrier.

He sent scouts searching for the best black ballplayers, keeping his true agenda a secret. Jackie was among the many athletes the scouts saw in action. They confirmed his speed, competitiveness, intelligence, and his uncanny abilities to bunt and to steal bases. His batting average in forty-seven games with the Monarchs was .387, with fourteen doubles, four triples, five home runs, and thirteen stolen bases. He had an awkward stance at home plate, but coaching could change that. At twenty-six, he was a little old, but the scouts believed that his natural talent and determination more than made up for his age.

Athletic prowess, however, was not Rickey's only criterion for the right candidate. Equally important was strength of character. From early childhood, Jackie had played with and competed against whites, so it would not be a new experience. His college years had given him the tools to analyze and evaluate challenges. His racial pride had compelled him to defy segregation in the army, which was proof of his courage. He was smart and tough. Rickey believed he had found his man.

The Dodger office was hot, almost as hot as it was outdoors. Branch Rickey was sitting in a leather swivel chair behind a massive mahogany desk. A giant stuffed elk head loomed on the wall behind him, along with photographs of Dodger manager Leo Durocher, Rickey's grandchildren and daughters, and a portrait of Abraham Lincoln. A lighted fish tank brightened up a sidewall. The goldfish swimming rapidly back and forth seemed to look as uneasy as Jackie felt.

Rickey had once played baseball himself, but the years had put bulk on the sixty-four-year-old manager. Even his fingers, holding an unlit cigar, were pudgy. He reached out, shook Jackie's hand, and stared at him from behind wire-rimmed glasses for a long time. Jackie stared back. Neither man spoke. Finally Rickey asked, "You got a girl?"

Jackie hesitated. *Why does he want to know that? It's*

none of his business. Jackie replied that he was engaged. Rickey then advised him to get married soon because, after today, he might need a woman at his side.

Why? Jackie thought, but he didn't ask.

Next, Rickey told Jackie that he wanted him to play for the Dodgers, becoming the first black ballplayer in the major leagues.

Jackie was speechless. The idea both thrilled and scared him.

Of course, Rickey explained, Jackie would first have to play for the Montreal Royals, the Dodgers' farm club in Canada, to prove that he was capable of competing in the majors. Even that would be a first, as there had never been a black minor-league player either. Before Jackie could respond, Rickey barked, "I know you're a good ballplayer. What I don't know is whether you have the guts."

It was unbelievable: Rickey questioning his courage! Before Jackie could respond, Rickey took off his jacket and launched into a performance of what life would be like for Jackie if he accepted the offer. Rickey played a hotel clerk refusing Jackie a room in the hotel where the other players were staying. Then he was a waiter, brusquely refusing to serve Jackie. He transformed himself into a fan screaming obscenities about Jackie, Jackie's parents, Jackie's wife. Rickey pretended to be a ballplayer on an opposing team, spiking Jackie as he ran the bases. He even swung a fist at

Jackie's head. They will do anything to make you lose your temper, Rickey explained. The physical and verbal abuse might be overwhelming. Could you control your temper? Rickey asked.

"Are you looking for a Negro who is afraid to fight back?" Jackie asked.

"Robinson," Rickey countered, "I'm looking for a ballplayer with guts enough not to fight back."

Rickey was asking Jackie to do something he had never done in his life. From the time he was little, Jackie had never backed down when confronted with racism. He did not believe that a person should be silent in the face of injustice. You had to let people know when something was unacceptable. That's why he had shouted at that little girl on Pepper Street and why he had challenged the police officer who didn't like the song that he and his friend were singing. That's why he had yelled at the provost marshal in Fort Riley, and why he had refused to back down on the bus at Fort Hood, and why he had punched the gas station attendant.

Yet Jackie knew that if black athletes were to ever break into the major leagues, someone had to be willing to do what Rickey was asking. It would change his life and Rachel's life for sure, but it could also change life for other black Americans.

"Yes," he finally answered.

12

THE JOURNEY OUT
FEBRUARY 28–29, 1946

Jackie and Rachel boarded the plane for the first leg of their trip from Los Angeles to the Montreal Royals training camp in Sanford, Florida. Branch Rickey had insisted that Rachel come, too, the only wife who would be allowed at training camp.

It had been only eighteen days since they had married. They had wanted a small, intimate wedding, but Rachel's mother had other ideas. Instead of the ceremony taking place in the small church Rachel belonged to, the service had been held in the Independent Church of Christ, one of the largest black churches in Los Angeles. The bride and groom were an elegant couple: Jackie in his black tuxedo and silk ascot, Rachel in a flowing white satin gown. At the pulpit surrounded by tall vases of gladiolas and other flowers, the Reverend Karl Downs had performed the ceremony.

Their wedding was of personal importance. Their journey to Sanford was of public importance, and they knew they would be on display for the entire coming year.

They were excited though nervous about what lay ahead. It was Rachel's first trip to the Deep South, and she knew there would be hardships. She worried that Jackie's temper might flare up. He had to be above reproach on and off the field, no matter what kind of abuse he might face. He had promised Rickey that he would keep his temper under control, but she knew how easily Jackie angered.

Except for the shoe box that Jackie carried, they were the height of fashion as they boarded the plane. Jackie wore a double-breasted blue suit with wide lapels and baggy pants. Rachel was wearing Jackie's wedding present, a dyed three-quarter-length ermine coat. A matching black hat and alligator-skin pocketbook completed her elegant outfit.

The shoe box, filled with fried chicken, boiled eggs, apples, and candy bars, was Mallie's good-bye gift. They hoped it wouldn't smell too much on the plane, but they would never have hurt her feelings by refusing her gift.

The all-night flight to New Orleans, their first layover,

was uneventful. But upon entering the terminal, Rachel felt bombarded by the "White" and "Colored" signs. It wasn't that Rachel was naive about racism. She had suffered her share in California. But it was not until now that she fully comprehended the humiliation and cruelty suffered every single day by black southerners. There wasn't even a bench for African Americans to sit on. Refusing to be cowed, she drank from a "White" water fountain. In the "White" ladies' room, women stared at her but said nothing. Their silence fortified her.

Jackie and Rachel were bumped from their next flight, to Pensacola, Florida, and told they couldn't get another until the following morning. They were exhausted and hungry. The airport restaurants were closed to blacks. Takeout was available, but there was no place to sit and eat. Jackie remembered a hotel that he had stayed at when traveling with the Monarchs. During the taxi ride over, they gratefully opened Mallie's shoe box of food, wondering if she had anticipated this very situation.

The hotel room was filthy, but exhaustion won over disgust, and they both fell asleep.

The next morning, they caught a flight to Pensacola. Upon arrival, they were told that their connection to Daytona Beach had been oversold: again, they couldn't get another flight until the following morning. Jackie confronted a flight attendant, asking why, if white people were boarding the plane, there wasn't enough room for them. The attendant explained that priority was being given to people booked from New Orleans; there was no room left for anyone booked out of Pensacola. Jackie knew it wasn't true and felt like yelling. He also knew that if he yelled, it would get into the newspapers, and the publicity would hurt his cause. Even worse, he could get himself and Rachel arrested, and Jackie knew what happened to black people arrested in the South. The Robinsons decided to skip flying altogether and take the next bus out of Pensacola to Jacksonville, where they would catch another bus to Daytona Beach. From there, they would be picked up and driven to the training camp.

Jackie and Rachel knew the drill: whites in the front of the bus, blacks in the back. Jackie hated it, but he would abide by it while he was in the South. They walked back to the last row of seats that reclined and settled in for the 357-mile trip and maybe some sleep. A few stops into the trip, the driver ordered them to move to the very last row. Since those seats did not recline, they would have to sit upright for the next sixteen hours. That would make sleep difficult. Jackie said not a word, and they moved. Rachel knew how humiliated and powerless he was feeling. She watched him fall asleep, then buried her head in her hands and cried.

The "Colored" waiting room in the Jacksonville bus

depot was hot and fly ridden. Jackie and Rachel hadn't eaten since New Orleans. Mallie's shoe box was empty. Jackie suggested buying food from a small place allotted for blacks, but Rachel refused. They waited for the bus to Daytona Beach.

On Saturday, March 2—after thirty-six hours of travel—the Robinsons arrived at Daytona Beach. The bus depot was exceptionally crowded, but photographer Bill Rowe and reporter Wendell Smith were there to drive them to the training camp, another forty miles away. Rickey had hired Smith to usher Jackie through the season, offering emotional support and help with any difficulties that might arise.

Knowing there would only be worse humiliations ahead, Jackie told the two men that he was ready to quit. Smith and Rowe listened and then quietly tried to convince him to stay. As they talked, Jackie grew vaguely aware that the crowd at the station had not thinned. Black and white people were milling about, trying to get a closer look at him. Then it dawned on him: these people were hanging around to see the man who was taking on the challenge of breaking the color barrier in Major League Baseball. That settled it—he wouldn't quit the team. He couldn't quit the team.

IN THE MINOR LEAGUES
MARCH 4–OCTOBER 4, 1946

Spring training in Sanford, Florida, was a blur of throwing, catching, and running and a buzz of friendly banter among more than one hundred and fifty ballplayers, each hoping to win a spot on the Montreal Royals. When Jackie stepped onto the field alongside John Richard Wright, the black pitcher newly signed by Rickey, the banter and activity stopped. Since Jackie had gotten the bulk of the publicity, the reporters pounced on him with the most questions. He fielded them with grace, though his stomach was in a knot.

Clay Hopper, Montreal's manager, came over to shake Jackie's hand. When he wasn't managing the Royals, Hopper was managing his plantation in Mississippi. Jackie was grateful for Hopper's handshake; many white southerners would never shake hands with a black person. Still, Jackie sensed some discomfort in Hopper's words of welcome. What Jackie did not know was that Hopper was vehemently opposed to him playing and had told Rickey not to sign him.

Two days into spring training, Rickey learned that a group of hostile whites in Sanford had demanded that the mayor oust Jackie from the city, and were planning a march to the house where the Robinsons were staying. Rickey quickly moved spring training to Daytona Beach. The white players settled into a luxurious hotel there, while Jackie and Rachel found themselves sleeping in a tiny bedroom in the home of a black family. All through the South, their lodgings would be at people's homes or at black hotels. Jackie hated this, but being angry about it wouldn't help. He needed to focus all his energy on playing.

As the training season progressed, there was more trouble. Officials in Jacksonville, Florida; Savannah, Georgia; Richmond, Virginia; and DeLand, Florida, refused to let the Royals play in their towns if Robinson and Wright took the field. Police in Sanford interrupted a game in the third inning and ordered Jackie off the field, citing a local law that prohibited blacks and whites from playing together on city property. Forced to sit in the Jim Crow section of the ballparks, Rachel was at every game, swallowing her own pride and anger.

The cancellations cost the team money, but Rickey pressed ahead as if that didn't bother him. He signed two new black players—twenty-year-old pitcher Don Newcombe and twenty-five-year-old catcher Roy Campanella—to another Dodger farm team.

As Rickey had predicted, Jackie drew hundreds of new spectators, including whites, to the games. Often there were not enough seats for all the black attendees who had traveled long distances to see Jackie play. The cheers of his black fans bolstered Jackie but pressured him, too. He had to succeed. If he could make it, they could make it. When he triumphed, they were empowered. He didn't want to let them down. He grew tense and overanxious.

Sometimes he swung at bad balls, desperate to get a hit. He pushed himself so hard fielding that his right arm grew sore. Hopper moved him from shortstop to second base to first base and then back to second, trying to find a position that required the least amount of throwing.

His coaches marveled at how fast he learned to play each position, but his hitting suffered. Jackie had been confident that he would make the Dodger lineup, but now he wondered if he would even be allowed to stay with the Royals. Every day without a hit made Rickey's experiment seem even more risky, yet Rickey seemed untroubled. He repeatedly encouraged Jackie to be daring on the field.

A few teammates reached out to share their baseball know-how with Jackie and John Wright. The rest, though cordial, were guarded. Jackie kept to himself, waiting for others to initiate conversation.

Prejudice followed Jackie and the Royals to their games in the North. In Syracuse, New York, the vitriol from the Chiefs' dugout was so vicious that the umpire ordered the game stopped until the name-calling ended. When the Royals were scheduled to play in Baltimore, the league president begged Rickey not to bring Robinson and Wright, predicting riots and violence. Rickey did not back down. The two teams played. There were no riots or violence, but from every part of the stadium throughout the three-game series, Baltimore fans booed and shouted racial epithets. Rachel thought perhaps it was time for Jackie to withdraw from the struggle.

April 18, 1946, marked the official opening of the International League season. Twenty-five thousand people crammed into Roosevelt Stadium in Jersey City to see the Montreal Royals face the Jersey City Giants, the farm team of the New York Giants. Thousands of black Americans had crossed the bridge from Harlem, in New York City, to see Jackie's debut. Hundreds had come from as far away as Philadelphia.

When Jackie came up to bat, his knees felt rubbery. His palms were so sweaty, he had trouble gripping the bat. On the sixth pitch, he hit a grounder and was thrown out at first. In the third inning, with men on first and second, he hit the ball 340 feet into the stands, bringing in three runs. As Jackie rounded third base, Montreal manager Clay Hopper patted him on the back. As he jogged to the dugout, his teammates rose to greet him.

Jackie was on a roll. In the fifth inning, he bunted, then stole second and got to third on a groundout by Tommy Tatum. When a new pitcher took his place on the mound, Jackie danced up and down the third-base line, threatening to steal home. The crowd lapped it up, but it rattled the pitcher so much that he stopped in mid-windup; the umpire declared the pitch a balk and sent Jackie home.

In the seventh inning, Jackie singled and stole second again, and in the eighth, he laid down another perfect bunt. Even Giants fans cheered the Royals' rookie that day. Montreal triumphed, 14–1, and swept the three-game series. Fans mobbed Jackie on the field and outside the stadium.

That season, thousands of black Americans followed the minor-league Royals across the country. In Louisville, Kentucky, so many turned out that the stadium's segregated section couldn't accommodate them all. People perched on the roofs of nearby buildings. Jackie's fans cheered when he stepped onto the field, and they cheered when he came to bat. They cheered when he got a hit and they cheered when he didn't.

The Canadians were even more enthusiastic. The Robinsons had no trouble finding a beautiful furnished apartment in Montreal. Neighbors who didn't speak a word of English nevertheless knocked on their door to welcome them. During home games, the Canadians shouted encouragement and praise. They greeted the Robinsons effusively in public and besieged Jackie in restaurants and on the street for autographs.

Such warm support did not, however, make up for the constant verbal battering on the road. The jeers and taunts were never-ending, but they were only one of the weapons used to unnerve Jackie. Manager Larry MacPhail of the New York Yankees' farm team ordered his pitchers to hit Jackie. Another manager offered to buy a suit for any pitcher who knocked Jackie down. The pitchers obliged, and Jackie was hit with a ball six times. When he wasn't hit, it was only because he got out of the way fast enough.

In the Royals' second series in Baltimore, the constant hostility affected Jackie's performance. In the first three games, he managed to get only two hits in ten times at bat. In the final game of the series, he regained his stride, getting three hits in three times at bat and scoring four runs to help the Royals to a 10–1 victory.

Jackie's fuse was just as short as ever. Many times he wanted to yell back, but he didn't. He would not break his promise to Rickey. He worked hard to keep his rage from showing on his face; every move he made was being watched.

By June, Jackie's dignity and skill had won his teammates over, but he couldn't sleep or eat. In August, the team doctor told him he was on the verge of a nervous breakdown and needed to rest for at least ten days. He took off only two days.

By the end of the season, Rickey's faith in Jackie's ability as an athlete and a role model was rewarded. Jackie went seventy-nine games without an error. He became the first Royal ever to win the league batting crown, with a .349 batting average. He ranked second in the league with forty stolen bases.

The 1946 Royals won the International League pennant by eighteen games. They were hailed as one of the greatest minor-league teams ever, and the sports world knew that Jackie Robinson had played a key role in the Royals' victory.

Pitcher John Wright, on the other hand, did not fulfill the potential that Rickey had initially seen in him and was let go from the Royals. Rickey hired a second black pitcher, but he was let go after two months.

On October 4, 1946, the Royals won the Little World Series, the contest for the championship of the minor leagues. Montrealers swooped down onto the field after the win and hoisted Jackie up on their shoulders. They hugged him, kissed him, and slapped him on the back. In the locker room, Clay Hopper congratulated him. "You're a great ballplayer and a fine gentleman," the manager said. "It's been wonderful having you on the team." An adoring crowd almost ripped the clothes off Jackie's back as he left the stadium. Reporter Sam Maltin of the *Pittsburgh Courier* wrote, "It was probably the only day in history that a black man ran from a white mob with love instead of lynching on its mind."

On November 18, five weeks after the season ended, Rachel and Jackie's first child, Jackie Jr., was born.

On April 10, 1947, the Brooklyn Dodgers officially announced that Jackie Roosevelt Robinson would be starting the 1947 major-league season as a Dodger.

14

BENCH JOCKEYING
APRIL–MAY 1947

Jackie had already left for Ebbets Field when Rachel packed up five-month-old Jackie Jr. and his baby gear and hailed a cab for Brooklyn. It was April 15, opening day of the 1947 Major League Baseball season and Jackie's first day in uniform as a Brooklyn Dodger. Jackie Jr. was getting over a bout of diarrhea, but after all they had been through so far, Rachel was determined not to miss the opening game.

At the stadium, Rachel ran around to find a hot dog vendor who would warm Jackie Jr.'s formula. Then she sat behind the Dodger dugout and immediately realized that the infant was inadequately dressed for the nippy day. Luckily she was sitting next to catcher Roy Campanella's mother-in-law, who snuggled the five-month-old inside her fur coat. That done, Rachel sat down to watch her twenty-eight-year-old husband make history.

Just shy of six feet tall, Jackie weighed 195 pounds. His shoulders seemed broad in comparison to his thin legs. His cap shielded his face from view, but the number on the back of his cream-and-blue flannel uniform—42—popped for all to see. Rachel didn't have to see Jackie's face to know how he felt about this moment. He had excelled with the Montreal Royals. Now came the big test, the one he could not afford to fail. It was a heavy weight to carry.

Cheers filled the stadium whenever Jackie came up to bat. In the first, third, and fifth innings, he didn't get a hit. In the bottom of the seventh, with the Dodgers trailing the Boston Braves, 3–2, Eddie Stanky, the Dodgers' second baseman, got on first with a walk. Jackie followed with a perfect sacrifice bunt, beat out the throw to first, and sailed to second on an error by the Braves' first baseman. Stanky advanced to third. Then Pete Reiser hit a double; Stanky and Jackie ran home, putting the Dodgers ahead, 4–3. Gene Hermanski drove in another run to clinch the win.

In his first week, Jackie played four games, got six hits out of fourteen times at bat, scored five times, and made thirty-three putouts without an error.

His teammates remained distant, but Jackie, like

Rickey, believed this would change. As he had done with the Montreal Royals, he kept to himself. He didn't ask to eat with his teammates, play cards with them, or sit near them. He even waited to shower until all the other players had finished.

What Jackie did not know was that before the regular season had even started, some of his teammates had drawn up a petition to keep him off the team. Most Dodger players were southern born and bred. Rickey knew how deeply ingrained their prejudice was, but he had no intention of tolerating racism. In private meetings, he told each petitioner that only *he* decided who played for the Dodgers. If someone didn't want to play with Jackie, Rickey would gladly trade him. Rickey was willing to lose even Dixie Walker, the team's leading hitter and most popular player.

"Bench jockeying" is a baseball tradition in which opposing teams shout insults at each other. Rookies got the worst of it, but no one was prepared for the vicious racial epithets thrown at Jackie on April 22, when the Philadelphia Phillies came to Ebbets Field. The Phillies' manager, Alabama-born Ben Chapman, had specifically instructed his players to taunt Jackie. It was common knowledge in the sports world that Jackie had promised Rickey that he would not respond to any attacks. From Jackie's first at bat to the end of the game, venom spewed from the Phillies dugout: "Hey, nigger, why don't you go back to the cotton field where you belong?" "They're waiting for you in the jungles, black boy!" "Go back to the bushes!"

The Phillies even heckled Jackie's teammates, telling them about all the diseases they would catch if they shared personal items with him. And there was worse, much worse. Never before had such hateful language been heard during a major-league game.

Jackie seethed. He wanted to drop his bat, run to the Phillies dugout, and slug it out. Why should he bear this? No one should bear this. *To hell with Mr. Rickey's "noble experiment,"* he thought. But too much was at stake for him and for his people, so he kept his eye on the ball.

The score was 0–0 in the bottom of the eighth inning when Jackie singled, then stole second, then third. A teammate singled, and Jackie raced home, scoring the game's only run for a Dodger triumph. Stealing bases had become one of Jackie's great weapons on the field.

The next day's game brought more abuse from the Phillies. This time the Dodgers' shortstop, Philadelphia-born Eddie Stanky, came to Jackie's defense. "Listen, you yellow-bellied cowards," he shouted, "why don't you yell at somebody who can answer back?"

Dodger fans seated near the Phillies dugout heard the slurs and protested to Commissioner Chandler, who in turn warned Chapman that if his team didn't stop the abuse, there would be punitive action.

On his Sunday radio program, newscaster Walter Winchell denounced Chapman. Sportswriters, black and white, criticized Chapman in print. Even Dodger Dixie Walker, who had not wanted to play alongside Jackie, told Chapman that he disapproved of what had happened.

Chapman met with black reporters and defended himself and his players, insisting they had done nothing wrong: they were simply engaging in the tradition of hazing that all rookies went through. He argued that in times past, players had been called all sorts of names—*wops, dagos, Polacks*—and no one had ever complained. Hank Greenberg, the first Jewish major-league player, was no stranger to the ethnic slurs *kike* and *sheenie.* The epithet *dago* was thrown at Joe Garagiola, who was of Italian descent. But sportswriters like Dan Parker of the *New York Daily Mirror* reminded their readers that Chapman was no stranger to charges of bigotry: in the past he had made many anti-Semitic remarks. Ironically, Chapman's behavior on and off the field helped unite the Dodgers in support of their newest rookie.

In the final two games with Philadelphia, Jackie fell into a slump, going 0–20 at bat. Jackie worried that the Dodgers' manager, Burt Shotton, might pull him out of the lineup, but Rickey's and Shotton's faith in him stood fast. They knew the slump would pass.

In May, Herb Pennock, the Phillies' general manager, telephoned Rickey and told him not to bring "the nigger" to the upcoming series in Philadelphia. Rickey informed Pennock that if the Phillies didn't want to play his team, the Dodgers would gladly accept that as a forfeit victory. Pennock dropped his threat.

Historically, the Dodgers stayed at the Benjamin Franklin Hotel whenever they were in Philadelphia. When they arrived there on May 9, the team was told that Jackie could not stay there. Wendell Smith found an all-black hotel for himself and Jackie.

Chapman, worried about his negative press, asked that Jackie pose for a photograph with him. The idea repulsed Jackie, but he knew it had to be done. The photograph shows Jackie and Chapman holding on to different ends of a baseball bat. Chapman had refused to shake Jackie's hand.

A newspaper reporter wrote that the St. Louis Cardinals were planning to strike if Jackie played in their upcoming series with the Dodgers. National League president Ford Frick declared, "This is the United States of America, and one citizen has as much right to play as another." He went on to announce that any player who went on strike would be suspended from the league. The rumored strike never materialized.

Commissioner Chandler's reprimand of the Phillies during the April series at first seemed to have an effect when the two teams met again in May. The verbal barrage was diminished. What took its place, however, was simply another show of contempt for Jackie: the Phillies pointed bats at him, making machine gun–like noises.

The Dodgers lost three of the four games and slipped out of first place, but Jackie's slump broke when he got three singles in eleven times at bat. In the third game, he hit his second home run of the season.

The doubleheader against the Phillies on May 11 boasted the largest crowd in the Phillies' history. Scalpers were selling two-dollar tickets for six dollars, the price of a World Series ticket.

On the road, attendance records were broken in Pittsburgh, Cincinnati, Chicago, and St. Louis. White Americans, dazzled by Jackie's speed and daring, flocked to see him play. Black families who had been loyal to the Negro leagues and had not previously attended major-league games in any great numbers traveled hundreds of miles to witness history.

When the Dodgers played in Cincinnati, a "Jackie Robinson special" train started six hundred miles away in Norfolk, Virginia, and stopped along the route to pick up black fans. After games, young and old gathered outside the stadiums, waiting and hoping to get Jackie's autograph.

Thousands more Americans tuned in on their radios to soak up Jackie's exploits.

Red Barber, the Dodgers' radio broadcaster, later declared what everyone by then knew was the truth: Jackie Robinson was "the biggest attraction in baseball since Babe Ruth."

In his column in the *Pittsburgh Courier,* Wendell Smith used a familiar nursery rhyme to describe the phenomenon:

Jackie's nimble
Jackie's quick
Jackie's making the turnstiles click.

15

STEALING HOME
JUNE 24, 1947

By late June, the Dodgers were in second place in the league, and Jackie's teammates knew he was a big factor in helping them get there. He was their top home run hitter, with a batting average around .300. He was among the National League's top hitters, run scorers, and base stealers. To capture the pennant, the Dodgers needed to win every game. Past glories didn't count.

On June 24, thirty-five thousand people packed Forbes Field in Pittsburgh. Fritz Ostermueller was on the mound for the Pirates. When the two teams had met earlier in June, Ostermueller hit Jackie on the left wrist with a fastball. It was the seventh time in two months that a pitcher had intentionally hit Jackie.

It was the top of the fifth. One out. The score was tied, 2–2. Ostermueller walked Dodger Al Gionfriddo. Jackie hit a grounder toward third and made it to first base, but Gionfriddo was beat out at second. Two outs. Carl Furillo hit a long drive to left field and sailed to first; Jackie raced off first and made it to third with ease.

Dodger slugger Dixie Walker was up. Ostermueller turned to check on Jackie, who was bouncing on his toes, dancing and prancing off third base as if ready to steal home the second Ostermueller took his eyes off him. Jackie's antics thrilled fans but drove pitchers crazy. It was hard to concentrate on your next pitch if you had to keep looking back or sideways to figure out what Jackie Robinson was going to do next.

Ostermueller was determined not to let Jackie unnerve him and turned his focus to striking out Walker. Besides, Jackie trying to steal home just didn't make any sense. As fast as Jackie was, Ostermueller's pitch would reach home plate before Jackie could, and the catcher would easily tag Jackie out.

Ostermueller threw his first pitch to Walker. Ball one. Pitch two: another ball. On the third pitch, Furillo took off and stole second. Jackie waited for Ostermueller's next pitch to Walker. He knew Ostermueller's windup was always slow, so as soon as the fourth pitch left his hand, Jackie streaked down the third-base line. The ball hit the catcher's mitt. The catcher reached out to tag Jackie, but it was too late. Jackie had slid in and scored, and the Dodgers took the lead, 3–2. In the top of the seventh, they expanded their lead to win the game, 4–2.

Seated near the Dodger dugout, Branch Rickey heard the crowd roar its delight and he chuckled to himself. Yes, he had chosen the right man, not just for his incredible athletic ability and dignity, but also for his fearlessness on the field.

16

THE PUBLIC SPEAKS
JULY 1947

Jackie stared at the huge pile of fan mail. There were many other letters, too: hate mail that threatened violence against him and his family. Unfortunately, the threatening letters were always sent anonymously, so the police couldn't track them.

All sorts of Americans, black and white, of different ages and backgrounds, from all parts of the country, wrote to Jackie. He was empowering black people and teaching white Americans that what mattered was talent, hard work, and character, not the color of a person's skin.

G. Gilbert Smith, the first African-American machinist to be hired in his factory of four hundred men, wrote:

> *I know what you are going thru because I went through the same thing in a much smaller way. . . . They did all the little dirty underhanded things to me that they must be doing to you. . . . I couldn't fight back because my side never would have been considered in a show down. . . . I know how much guts it takes to go out on that field and play the kind of ball you're playing under such pressure. . . . If I can raise my boy to be half the man that you are, I'll be a happy father.*

T. S. Washington, a bellman at the Eaton Hotel in Wichita, Kansas, wrote:

> *Saw you play in Wichita and also in St. Louis . . . and decided that I wanted to name my expected child for the first Negro in league baseball. And above that a good sport and a gentleman, something our race needs as bad as they do a square deal. Little Jackie Lee was born 8-15-47–2 pm (a girl).*

Letters of support came from some unexpected places, too:

I happen to be a white Southerner . . . rooting for you to make good. . . . I know that very few of us whites can understand the terrific pressure put on you—but I know, at least, that you are doing every bit as good a job for your race as a Booker T. Washington, a George Washington Carver, or a Marian Anderson. I should also say that you're doing a darned fine job for all Americans. Stick to it, kid. . . . You've got a lot more friends in this country of ours than enemies.

Sixth-graders from Connecticut wrote to Commissioner Chandler, reminding him of America's promise of equality:

Not all of us are Dodger fans but we still think that Jackie Robinson should play on any Major team in the Leagues. All who are Americans have equal rights as . . . citizens and should be able to do as others can do, even if his race is different. We all are born the same, eat the same, and sleep the same, why can't we play the same? Why not give everyone an equal chance?

That July, three more black athletes—Larry Doby for the Cleveland Indians and Hank Thompson and Willard Brown for the St. Louis Browns—were signed. It seemed integration in the majors was here to stay.

17

AN ALONE LIFE
JULY–AUGUST 1947

Jackie's teammates knew the constant pressure he was under, and they witnessed his dignity and courage in facing it. Pitchers were still intentionally hitting him. The abusive language had not stopped, but still he kept focused on the game. Even though Jackie had a grand mission, he wasn't out for personal glory. When he stole bases, it was to win, not to rack up statistics and applause. He was a team player. His incredible talent was helping move the team toward capturing the National League pennant. He had earned their respect and gratitude. Now he was invited to join in the banter and card games, but still, there was no player he could really call a friend.

He was welcomed in Pittsburgh, Boston, and Chicago hotels, but he was still barred from the Benjamin Franklin Hotel in Philadelphia and all hotels in St. Louis. Cincinnati's Netherland Plaza now agreed to let him stay, but wouldn't let him eat in the hotel restaurant or swim in its pool. Not one teammate objected on his behalf. No player ever invited him to go out to eat somewhere else. Most nights he ate alone or with Wendell Smith.

On the playing field, the racist taunts had not stopped. In St. Louis, on July 29, as hateful words echoed around the Cardinals' stadium, Jackie's fans came to his defense. Black spectators were the first to stand up and applaud him. Soon whites were standing and cheering him on, too. The whistling and shouting got so loud that it drowned out the jeering and the vile language. As heartening as his fans' support was, it could not erase Jackie's persistent aloneness.

When he was home in Brooklyn with Rachel and Jackie Jr., love surrounded him, but the tension inside him never completely disappeared. Black Americans were depending on him to succeed, to show the white world that they were equally talented if given the chance. It was an overwhelming and constant burden. It disturbed his sleep. Oftentimes it made him uncommunicative.

Branch Rickey had been right when he told Jackie that he would need a good woman by his side. Rachel was that loving, understanding woman. She knew not to probe, to give him room to be silent and reflect. She was there, waiting patiently to listen whenever he was ready to talk. He was a lucky man.

18

THE FINAL STRETCH
AUGUST–SEPTEMBER 1947

By early August, it looked as if the Dodgers would win the National League pennant, but in mid-August the Cardinals began racking up wins as their powerhouse hitters, Stan Musial and Enos Slaughter, found their stride again. The rivalry between the two teams was fierce. The year before, the Cardinals had beaten the Dodgers in the playoffs for the pennant. The Dodgers were determined not to let that happen again.

In August, in a four-game series between the two teams, the Dodgers won the first and second games but lost the third.

Both teams needed this last win, but after ten innings and three hours, the score was still tied. In the top of the eleventh, Musial got on first. Then Slaughter hit a low fastball right toward Jackie on first base. Jackie scooped it up for an easy out, then shot a glance at second to see if he could throw Musial out. He couldn't, so he turned back to first, only to see Slaughter still barreling toward him. Slaughter deliberately ran into Jackie, stepping on Jackie's left foot, the spikes of his cleat gashing the back of Jackie's heel. Jackie dropped to the ground. The pain was excruciating. After a minute or so, he hopped back up, grabbed his ankle, and called time-out. Slaughter walked casually back to the dugout.

A few infuriated Dodgers ran onto the field to protest. This was the second spiking of Jackie in this series. In the first game, Joe Medwick had spiked him, but no one believed it was intentional. There was no doubt that Slaughter's spiking was deliberate. He had had plenty of room to land on the bag without touching Jackie. A few more inches, and Jackie's Achilles tendon would have been severed and his baseball career over. In spite of being hurt, Jackie finished the game. The Dodgers lost, but Slaughter's aggression and his denial that he had deliberately spiked Jackie made the Dodgers even more determined to triumph over the Cardinals.

On September 11, the two teams met again. With only

sixteen games left in the season, the Dodgers' first-place lead was small—only four and a half games.

In the bottom of the second inning, Cardinal catcher Joe Garagiola, trying to outrun a double play, spiked Jackie's left foot when he reached first base. In the top of the third inning, when Jackie came up to bat, he made some remark to Garagiola. The catcher reacted by standing up and spitting out a racist epithet. Jackie lost his temper and made a move toward Garagiola. Garagiola threw down his mask. More words were exchanged. The fans in the stadium anticipated a fight. The umpire stepped in to calm the situation. Coach Clyde Sukeforth rushed from the Dodger dugout and pulled Jackie away from Garagiola, and the game continued. Jackie popped out, ending the inning.

Jackie's chance for payback came in the top of the fifth inning. With two out, he hit a two-run homer to tie the score. In the top of the eighth, Cookie Lavagetto's long drive into left field clinched a 4–3 win for the Dodgers.

In the final game of the series, with two out in the bottom of the eighth, Jackie chased a foul pop toward the Dodger dugout, determined to make the catch. Reaching the dugout, he had no more room to run, so he hurled himself down the dugout steps to get the ball. Teammate Ralph Branca, seeing that Jackie was going to fall on the concrete floor of the dugout, leaped up from the bench. Jackie caught the ball just as Branca grabbed him around his waist to break his fall and push him back onto the soft infield grass. Jackie's teammates rushed to congratulate him on his extraordinary catch and to praise Branca for *his* extraordinary catch. The sight of a white man protecting a black man was startling, as friendly physical contact between whites and blacks was virtually nonexistent at this time in American history.

The Dodgers went on to win the game, 8–7.

19

THE TRIUMPHANT RETURN
LATE SEPTEMBER 1947

The Dodgers clinched the pennant—their first in six years—on September 22, but Brooklynites didn't wait for the official end of the 1947 season to celebrate. On September 19, three thousand ecstatic fans greeted the team at Pennsylvania Station as they returned from their road trip. As in Montreal, fans mobbed Jackie. He managed to outrun them to a telephone booth to call Rachel. Six police officers cleared a path to the subway for Jackie so he could get home to Rachel and Jackie Jr.

September 23 was declared Jackie Robinson Day at

Ebbets Field. Jackie's mother, taking her first airplane flight, attended, along with thirty-two thousand other people. J. G. Taylor Spink, the publisher of *Sporting News,* who had spoken out against integrating Major League Baseball, presented Jackie with his paper's very first Rookie of the Year award. Spink stated clearly that Jackie was not getting the award for being a trailblazer but for his superb skills.

Jackie's batting average for the season was .297. He led the Dodgers with 125 runs scored and led the league with twenty-nine stolen bases. In forty-six tries at bunting, he had failed only four times to reach first base. He tied teammate Dixie Walker for the most doubles and Pee Wee Reese for the most home runs. Walker, one of the Dodgers' most vociferous opponents of Jackie playing for the team, said, "No other ballplayer on this club with the possible exception of [catcher] Bruce Edwards has done more to put the Dodgers up in the race than Robinson has. He is everything Branch Rickey said he was when he came up from Montreal."

During the 1947 season, almost 1.9 million people had paid to see the Dodgers on the road. At Ebbets Field, which seated only thirty-two thousand people, 1.8 million fans had come to home games.

In a nationwide contest of the most respected men in America, Jackie was ahead of President Truman and World

War II heroes General Dwight D. Eisenhower and General Douglas MacArthur. He came in second only to pop singer Bing Crosby. *Time* magazine put Jackie on its cover. He received countless invitations to speak all over the country. A movie about his life was planned.

20

THE SUBWAY SERIES
SEPTEMBER 30–OCTOBER 6, 1947

New York City was a flurry of excitement. Two home teams—the Brooklyn Dodgers and the New York Yankees—were facing off in the World Series. The Yankees had captured the American League pennant by twelve games. The Dodgers had beat out the Cardinals in the National League by five games.

Americans, black and white, from all over the country had booked trains and airplanes and gassed up their cars to get to the city. New York's hotels were booked solid. Jackie's mother, Rachel's mother, Jackie's brother Mack, his sister Willa, the Reverend Karl Downs, and five of Mack's friends had flown in from California. Yankee baseball great

Babe Ruth, entertainer Danny Kaye, New York governor Thomas E. Dewey, and New York City's mayor, William O'Dwyer, were among the 73,365 fans packed into Yankee Stadium for the first game. Another twenty-five thousand or so were seated on nearby rooftops. The series was set to boom out from the eighty million radios in the country, and for the first time, more than 3.9 million people would watch a World Series on television in their homes or in bars. President Harry Truman had said he hoped to find some time to watch it.

Most sportswriters had declared that the Yankees were a superior team and would take the series in four or at most five games. Dodger manager Burt Shotton encouraged his players not to be intimidated by these predictions. They, too, were a great team. They had triumphed over the powerful hitters of the Giants and the Cardinals, and faced down the great pitchers of the Boston Braves.

The Yankees were concerned about Jackie. They had to figure out how to control him. Their pitchers couldn't just walk him, because once on base he was a terror. Jackie's season record was twenty-nine steals, more than the whole Yankee team combined.

In the first inning of the first game, however, Yankee pitcher Frank Shea walked Jackie. Then Pete Reiser came up to bat, and on Shea's second pitch, Jackie streaked off for second and beat out the throw. Reiser hit a hard grounder, and Jackie bolted for third. Shea scooped up the ball, and the fans watched spellbound as Jackie stopped and faked with his head and shoulders as if he were going to return to second. His strategy worked. Shea was confused about where Jackie was headed and tossed the ball to second baseman Phil Rizzuto. The ball flew over Rizzuto's head, and Jackie resumed his race toward third. He was tagged out, but all the back-and-forth had allowed Reiser to get safely to second, in position to bring in a run. And when Dixie Walker hit a long fly to left field, Reiser raced home, and the Dodgers took the lead. The Dodgers did not win this first game, but Jackie Robinson gave the fans a mighty show.

When the Yankees won the second game, many predicted they would go on to sweep the series. Then the Dodgers came back to win the next two games. In the fifth game, Jackie drove in the lone Dodger run, but the win went to the Yankees. The Dodgers came back with a victory in the sixth game, tying up the series again, but the Yankees took the seventh and final game to win the World Championship of 1947.

The Yankees had triumphed, but all of Brooklyn was proud of their Dodgers anyway, and especially proud of Jackie Robinson.

21

42 IS NOT JUST A NUMBER

APRIL 15, 1997

For ten years, Jackie Robinson dazzled baseball fans with his fielding, hitting, and speed. He helped the Dodgers win six pennants and one World Series. In 1949, he led the National League in stolen bases, double plays, and batting average. He was the first African American named the league's Most Valuable Player.

On July 23, 1962, Jackie became the first black ballplayer inducted into the Baseball Hall of Fame. In his acceptance speech, he thanked the three most important people in his life: his mother, Mallie; his wife, Rachel; and Branch Rickey.

Jackie Robinson died in 1972 at age fifty-three.

On April 15, 1997, fifty years to the day after Jackie

Robinson broke the color barrier in Major League Baseball, Shea Stadium was packed for a game between the New York Mets and the Los Angeles Dodgers. President Bill Clinton, Ralph Branca, and Larry Doby were there, along with fifty-four thousand fans. Jackie's grandson Jesse Robinson Simms threw out the first ball.

The game was stopped halfway through, and all eyes were on Rachel Robinson, Sharon Robinson (Jackie and Rachel's daughter), Jesse Robinson Simms, and Branch Rickey as they walked to Jackie's position near second base.

President Clinton spoke first: "It's hard to believe that it was fifty years ago that a twenty-eight-year-old rookie changed the face of baseball and the face of America forever. Jackie Robinson scored the go-ahead run that day; we've all been trying to catch up ever since. . . . If Jackie Robinson were here today, he would say we have done a lot of good in the last fifty years, but we could do a lot better."

Rachel Robinson also reminded the fans that there was still work to be done. "I believe the greatest tribute we can pay to Jackie Robinson is to gain new support for a more equitable society, and in this heady environment of unity it is my hope that we can carry this living legacy beyond this glorious moment."

Acting baseball commissioner Bud Selig declared Jackie Robinson "bigger than the game." His voice booming through the loudspeakers, Selig then made a surprise announcement: "Number forty-two belongs to Jackie Robinson for the ages."

No new player in either the major or minor leagues would ever be allowed to wear the number 42 again.

Every year, April 15 is Jackie Robinson Day in Major League Baseball. Players on every team in both leagues don a uniform with the number 42 on the back to remember and honor the man who changed baseball and American history forever.

AUTHOR'S NOTE

I was eight years old in 1947, the first year that Jackie Robinson played for the Dodgers. Two years later, I became interested in baseball and turned into an avid Dodgers fan. Every night when my father came through the front door, I grabbed the *New York Post* from him and went first to the baseball statistics in the back of the paper, tracking the previous day's plays by my beloved Dodgers. I knew all the players' names and positions and could reel off their statistics without hesitation.

My father had absolutely no interest in any sport, so I was continually surprised that he would ask how the Dodgers were doing, how Jackie Robinson was doing. Many years later, I realized that it was Jackie Robinson the man who was the focus of my father's interest and admiration. My father perceived and understood his courage, recognized his significance in American history, and was pulling for him.

Jackie Robinson helped transform white Americans' consciousness and views about the abilities and rights of American blacks. He was a beacon of hope for black Americans in an era of extremely limited opportunities. In the magnificent civil rights movement of the 1960s, which also changed American history, tens of thousands of black Americans marched and took part in sit-ins, taking strength and courage from one another. Jackie Robinson, however, forged a path alone. He was a one-person civil rights movement. My father understood that and was cheering on the ballplayer in a way that was very different from the way his ten-year-old daughter was.

TIME LINE

January 31, 1919 Jack Roosevelt "Jackie" Robinson is born in Cairo, Georgia, to Jerry and Mallie Robinson.

May 21, 1920 Mallie Robinson leaves Georgia for Pasadena, California, taking her five children—Edgar (10), Frank (9), Mack (6), Willa Mae (4), and Jackie (16 months)—with her.

Early 1935 Sixteen-year-old Jackie finishes at Washington Junior High and enrolls at the John Muir Technical High School, which Mack and Willa Mae already attend.

July 18, 1936 Matthew "Mack" Robinson wins a silver medal in the 1936 Berlin Olympics, behind Jesse Owens, in the 200-meter dash.

February 1937–February 1939 Jackie attends Pasadena Junior College.

January 1938 Jackie meets the Reverend Karl Everette Downs.

1939 Jackie's brother Frank Robinson dies in a motorcycle accident.

February 15, 1939–March 3, 1941 Jackie attends the University of California at Los Angeles (UCLA).

September 1940 Jackie meets Rachel Isum at UCLA.

Fall 1941 Jackie works construction in Honolulu, Oahu, Hawaii, during the day and plays football at night for the Honolulu Bears.

December 5, 1941 Jackie leaves Hawaii.

December 7, 1941 The Japanese bomb Pearl Harbor, and the United States is plunged into war.

March 23, 1942 Jackie is drafted into the U.S. Army.

April 3, 1942 Jackie reports to Fort Riley, Kansas, for basic training.

January 28, 1943 Jackie receives the rank of second lieutenant in a cavalry of the U.S. Army.

August 2, 1944 Jackie is court-martialed at Camp Hood, Texas, for insubordination. He is found not guilty of all charges.

November 28, 1944 Jackie receives an honorable discharge from the army.

March 12, 1945 The Ives-Quinn Act passes.

March–August 1945 Jackie plays for the Kansas City Monarchs in the Negro baseball league.

June 1, 1945 Rachel graduates from UCLA with honors and a BS in nursing.

October 23, 1945 Jackie signs to play with the Montreal Royals, a Brooklyn Dodgers farm team.

February 10, 1946 Rachel and Jackie are married in Los Angeles.

March–October 1946 Jackie plays one season for the Montreal Royals.

November 18, 1946 Jackie Robinson Jr. is born.

April 10, 1947 Brooklyn Dodgers manager Branch Rickey buys Jackie's Montreal contract.

April 15, 1947 Jackie becomes the first black player in Major League Baseball.

Fall 1949 Jackie is named the National League's Most Valuable Player.

January 13, 1950 Jackie and Rachel's daughter, Sharon Annetta Robinson, is born.

May 14, 1952 Jackie and Rachel's second son, David Robinson, is born.

1956 Jackie is traded to the New York Giants but decides to retire from Major League Baseball. He becomes a vocal supporter of the civil rights movement.

January 14, 1957 Jackie is named vice president of personnel relations at Chock full o'Nuts.

July 23, 1962 Jackie is inducted into the Baseball Hall of Fame.

January 4, 1965 Jackie cofounds Freedom National Bank, the largest black-owned and operated bank in New York State at the time.

1965 Rachel is appointed assistant professor of nursing at Yale University School of Nursing and serves as the director of nursing for the state mental health center in New Haven, Connecticut.

June 17, 1971 Jackie Jr. dies in a car accident.

October 24, 1972 Jack Roosevelt Robinson dies of a heart attack at age fifty-three.

1973 Rachel creates the Jackie Robinson Foundation, which provides college scholarships to minority students.

August 2, 1982 Jackie Robinson becomes the first Major League Baseball player to appear on a U.S. postage stamp.

March 26, 1984 Jackie Robinson is posthumously awarded the Presidential Medal of Freedom.

April 15, 1997 Jackie Robinson's jersey number, 42, is retired from baseball in perpetuity.

SOURCE NOTES

In researching this biography, I read many different sources to present the most accurate portrayal of Jackie Robinson's life and to assure that my telling of his story would contain nothing invented. Jackie Robinson wrote about his life and also gave many interviews about his feelings and thoughts, which is how I am able to share them with you. Throughout this book you will find quotes from Robinson and other people. In some instances, the quotes have been shortened without changing an iota of their meaning. Words or sentences that have been left out are indicated by ellipses. Some punctuation has been simplified.

In the course of my research, I also read well-documented biographies of Jackie Robinson and Branch Rickey (and even studied their footnotes); interviews with Jackie's wife, Rachel Robinson; and many newspaper and magazine articles. These sources helped me re-create various events in his life without fictionalizing. An invaluable website source, baseball-almanac.com, with its play-by-play descriptions of all the Dodger games in the 1947 season, helped me accurately re-create those games. In reading the different sources, I sometimes found contradictory statements about events, statistics, or what various people said; I compared the sources to determine what I believed to be the truth.

Chapter One: The Neighborhood, 1927

p. 4: "Nigger, nigger, nigger" and "cracker": quoted in Robinson, Duckett, p. 5.

Chapter Three: "International Day," Summer 1934

p. 10: if she wanted "to get closer to heaven," she should visit California: quoted in Rampersad, p. 16.

Chapter Four: Mack's Big Challenge, July 18, 1936

Mack Robinson attended the University of Oregon, where he continued to pile up awards in NCAA, AAU, and Pacific Coast Conference track meets. He graduated from the university in 1941. In the opening ceremony of the 1984 Olympic Games, he was one of six Olympic champions who carried the giant Olympic flag into the Los Angeles Memorial Coliseum.

As a truant officer at John Muir Technical High School and an advocate against street crime, Mack Robinson pressed the Pasadena city government to provide better programs and facilities for young people.

Pasadena finally acknowledged Mack's and Jackie's achievements in 1997 with a sculpture of the two brothers in Centennial Square, and in 2000 by dedicating the Pasadena City College stadium to Mack. That same year, the United States Postal Service named the new branch at 600 Lincoln Avenue in Pasadena the Matthew "Mack" Robinson Post Office.

Chapter Five: A New Path, January 1938

p. 16: "Is Jack Robinson here?" and "Tell him I want to see him at the junior church": quoted in Rampersad, p. 52.

p. 18: He so wanted to ease her financial burden . . . but he felt uncertain about staying in college: In his autobiography, *I Never Had It Made,* Jackie Robinson wrote that "one of the frustrations of my teens was watching Mother work so hard. I wanted to help more, but I knew how much my college education meant to her. It seemed impossible to earn enough part-time for college expenses and still be able to provide money to relieve her of her daily grind." He also wrote, "It seemed very necessary for me to relieve some of my mother's financial burdens even though I knew it had always been her dream to have me finish college." Robinson, Duckett, pp. 8, 11.

Chapter Six: University Life, February 1939–March 1941

p. 21: Jackie didn't want to go that far from home: Robinson, Duckett, p. 10.

p. 23: She had seen him play at Pasadena Junior College and thought him conceited, but his smile and confidence warmed her to him now . . . a straight-A student: Rampersad, pp. 78–79.

p. 24: It felt good to be sending money to his mother: In an interview, Jackie's friend Ray Bartlett, who was also in Hawaii, told Robinson's biographer Arnold Rampersad, "We could use the extra money, because we were both trying to help our mothers." Quoted in Rampersad, p. 86.

Chapter Seven: From Private to Lieutenant, July–August 1942

p. 27: "I'll break up the team before I'll have a nigger on it": quoted in Rampersad, p. 91.

p. 27: "I don't want nobody to call me champ until I beat Schmeling": the official site of Joe Louis, www.cmgww.com/sports/louis/bio.htm.

p. 29: "Lieutenant, let me put it . . . . nigger?": quoted in Robinson, Duckett, p. 14.

p. 29: Jackie shouted back . . . nigger: ibid., p. 14.

Chapter Eight: The Confrontation, July 6–November 28, 1944

p. 33: "That's all right," "I don't care," and "This nigger is making trouble": quoted in Rampersad, p. 102.

p. 33: "Nobody comes into the room until I tell him": ibid., p. 103.

p. 34: "an uppity nigger" and "had no right to speak to that lady in that manner": Robinson, Duckett, p. 20.

p. 34: "I feel I have as much right . . . ask questions": ibid.

p. 35: "I am a Negro" and "not a nigger": quoted in Rampersad, p. 108.

p. 35: "simply a situation in which . . . as a soldier": ibid., p. 109.

p. 36: He appealed again, explaining . . . his old football injury: ibid., pp. 110–111.

p. 36: "honorably relieved from active duty . . . by reason of physical disqualification": ibid., p. 111.

Chapter Nine: In the Negro Leagues, March–August 1945

p. 38: But right now, Jackie didn't want to listen . . . Jackie was so tired, he played while half asleep: Jackie Robinson wrote a lot about the humiliating life in the Negro leagues and on the road. He wrote about how much the other players taught him, but there were times he was too exhausted to listen to anyone. All of the players were constantly exhausted. Any players who wrote about being in the Negro leagues wrote about the extreme fatigue.

p. 39: "Yours is over there" and "What do you mean my bathroom? There's a bathroom right here": quoted in Falkner, p. 94.

p. 39: His teammates warned him . . . they might not have gotten away alive: Tygiel, p. 63.

Chapter Ten: Advocating for Change, 1937–1947

p. 41: Wendell Smith is mentioned in all major biographies of Jackie Robinson for his groundbreaking newspaper articles focusing on integrating Major League Baseball and for his personal relationship with Jackie. He was posthumously inducted into the writers' wing of the Baseball Hall of Fame in 1994.

p. 43: "There is no rule . . . teams of organized ball": quoted in Tygiel, p. 38.

p. 44: Jackie was disgusted . . . miles for nothing: Falkner, p. 102.

p. 44: "What a ballplayer! Too bad he's the wrong color": quoted in Rampersad, p. 120.

p. 44: "I don't believe in barring Negroes from baseball just because they are Negroes": quoted in Tygiel, p. 43.

p. 45: "I'm more for your cause . . . defeating your own aims": ibid., p. 46.

p. 45: "rackets": ibid., p. 47.

p. 45: "It would be a hot day . . . organized [white] baseball": ibid. A slightly different version of this quote can be found in Rowan, p. 104.

Chapter Eleven: The Interview, August 28, 1945

p. 46: Rickey was interested in creating a new "colored" team, which he would call the Brooklyn Brown Dodgers: Trying to keep his real agenda of integrating baseball a secret, Branch Rickey offered William A. "Gus" Greenlee, who wanted to start a new Negro league, the use of Ebbets Field for Greenlee's team, the Brooklyn Brown Dodgers. The team played only one season—1946—at Ebbets.

p. 47: The acute emotional pain and humiliation that Thomas suffered that night still haunted Rickey: Tygiel, p. 52. Rickey retold the story of Charles Thomas many times throughout his life. He tended to tell it melodramatically, so I have toned it down for the purpose of representing the truth at the heart of his story. In an interview with Tygiel, however, Rickey's exact word was "haunted."

pp. 47–48: Rickey's moral commitment to integrating the majors . . . a place for himself in the history books: Branch Rickey was a complex, larger-than-life personality who loved attention and enjoyed press conferences. All sportswriters agreed that his motives for wanting to integrate the majors were many.

p. 48: They confirmed his speed . . . uncanny abilities to bunt and steal bases: Tygiel, p. 59.

p. 49: "You got a girl?": quoted in Robinson, Duckett, p. 30.

pp. 49–50: *Why does he want to know that? It's none of his business:* "It was a hell of a question. . . . Why should he be concerned about my relationship with a girl?": ibid., p. 30.

p. 50: "I know you're a good ballplayer . . . whether you have the guts": ibid., p. 31.

p. 51: "Are you looking for a Negro who is afraid to fight back?": ibid., p. 33.

p. 51: "Robinson . . . I'm looking for a ballplayer with guts enough not to fight back": ibid.

Chapter Twelve: The Journey Out, February 28–29, 1946

pp. 52–56: The thoughts and feelings attributed to Rachel Robinson and Jackie Robinson in this chapter are based on Rampersad's interviews with Rachel Robinson. Rampersad, pp. 136–138.

Chapter Thirteen: In the Minor Leagues, March 4–October 4, 1946

p. 58: Jackie hated this. . . . He needed to focus all his energy on playing: Based on a quote Tygiel found in an undated clipping in the Jackie Robinson papers, which read, "Plenty of times I wanted to haul off when somebody insulted me for the color of my skin. But I had to hold to myself. I knew I was kind of an experiment. . . . The whole thing was bigger than me": Tygiel, p. 192.

pp. 58–59: Forced to sit in the Jim Crow section of the ballparks, Rachel was at every game, swallowing her own pride and anger: ibid., p. 122.

p. 60: Rachel thought perhaps it was time for Jackie to withdraw from the struggle: ibid.

p. 61: When Jackie came up to bat . . . trouble gripping the bat: Descriptions of Jackie's state of mind during that April 18, 1946, game between the Montreal Royals and the Jersey City Giants can be found in many articles.

p. 62: Another manager offered to buy a suit for any pitcher who knocked Jackie down: Tygiel, p. 133.

p. 63: Jackie's fuse was just as short as ever. Many times he wanted to yell back, but he didn't: ibid., p. 192.

p. 63: he couldn't sleep or eat . . . needed to rest for at least ten days: ibid., p. 139.

p. 64: "You're a great ballplayer . . . wonderful having you on the team": quoted in Robinson, Duckett, p. 52.

p. 64: "It was probably the only day . . . lynching on its mind": quoted in Tygiel, p. 143.

Chapter Fourteen: Bench Jockeying, April–May 1947

pp. 65–66: At the stadium, Rachel. . . . her fur coat: Rampersad, p. 169.

p. 68: "Hey, nigger . . . where you belong?," "They're waiting . . . black boy!," and "Go back to the bushes!": quoted in Robinson, Duckett, p. 58.

p. 68: *To hell with Mr. Rickey's "noble experiment"*: ibid., pp. 58–59.

p. 68: "Listen, you yellow-bellied . . . who can answer back?": ibid., p. 60.

p. 69: Chapman met with black reporters . . . no one had ever complained: Falkner, p. 164, and Tygiel, p. 183.

p. 70: "the nigger": quoted in Rampersad, p. 175.

p. 70: Chapman, worried . . . he knew it had to be done: Jackie downplayed what had happened with the Phillies in interviews at that time. Years later, he admitted, "I can think of no occasion where I had more difficulty in swallowing my pride and doing what seemed best for baseball and the cause of the Negro in baseball than in agreeing to pose for a photograph with a man for whom I had only the very lowest regard": quoted in Rowan, p. 184.

On the sixty-ninth anniversary of Jackie Robinson's first game with the Dodgers, the city council of Philadelphia passed a resolution naming every April 15 in honor of Jackie Robinson and officially apologized for the racist treatment Robinson experienced in the April 1947 series with the Philadelphia Phillies.

p. 70: "This is the United States of America, and one citizen has as much right to play as another": quoted in Tygiel, p. 186.

p. 72: "the biggest attraction in baseball since Babe Ruth": quoted in Rampersad, p. 170.

p. 72: "Jackie's nimble . . . the turnstiles click": quoted in Tygiel, p. 189.

Chapter Fifteen: Stealing Home, June 24, 1947

p. 74: Ostermueller was determined . . . turned his focus to striking out Walker: Eig, p. 167.

Chapter Sixteen: The Public Speaks, July 1947

p. 77: "I know what you are going thru . . . I'll be a happy father": quoted in Eig, pp. 106–107.

p. 77: "Saw you play in Wichita . . . Little Jackie Lee was born 8-15-47–2 pm (a girl)": quoted in Falkner, p. 180.

p. 78: "I happen to be a white Southerner . . . You've got a lot more friends in this country of ours than enemies": quoted in Eig, p. 107.

p. 78: "Not all of us are Dodger fans . . . Why not give everyone an equal chance?": ibid., p. 108.

Chapter Seventeen: An Alone Life, July–August 1947

pp. 80–81: It was an overwhelming . . . made him uncommunicative: Robinson, Duckett, pp. 54, 62; Rampersad, p.180.

Chapter Nineteen: The Triumphant Return, Late September 1947

p. 87: Spink stated clearly that Jackie . . . his superb skills: Rampersad, p. 180.

p. 87: "No other ballplayer on this club . . . came up from Montreal": quoted in Rampersad, pp. 185–186.

p. 87: The statistics for attendance at Dodgers home games in 1947 come from baseball-reference.com. The exact number the site notes is 1,807,527.

Chapter Twenty-One: 42 Is Not Just a Number, April 15, 1997

p. 93: "It's hard to believe that it was fifty years ago . . . but we could do a lot better": quoted in Claire Smith, "A Grand Tribute to Robinson and His Moment," *New York Times,* April 16, 1997.

p. 93: "I believe the greatest tribute . . . we can carry this living legacy beyond this glorious moment": ibid.

pp. 93–94: "bigger than the game. . . . Number forty-two belongs to Jackie Robinson for the ages": ibid.

SELECTED BIBLIOGRAPHY

Eig, Jonathan. *Opening Day: The Story of Jackie Robinson's First Season*. New York: Simon & Schuster, 2007.

Erskine, Carl. *What I Learned from Jackie Robinson: A Teammate's Reflections On and Off the Field*. With Burton Rocks. New York: McGraw-Hill, 2005.

Falkner, David. *Great Time Coming: The Life of Jackie Robinson, from Baseball to Birmingham*. New York: Simon & Schuster, 1995.

Goldstein, Richard. *Spartan Seasons: How Baseball Survived the Second World War*. New York: Macmillan, 1980.

Kahn, Roger. *The Boys of Summer*. New York: Harper & Row, 1972.

Lowenfish, Lee. *Branch Rickey: Baseball's Ferocious Gentleman*. Lincoln: University of Nebraska Press, 2007.

Plaschke, Bill. "As Jackie Robinson Was Making History, Wendell Smith Wrote It." *Los Angeles Times*, April 14, 2013.

Polner, Murray. *Branch Rickey: A Biography*. New York: Atheneum, 1982.

Rampersad, Arnold. *Jackie Robinson: A Biography*. New York: Knopf, 1997.

Robinson, Jackie. *First Class Citizenship: The Civil Rights Letters of Jackie Robinson*. Edited by Michael G. Long. New York: Times Books, 2007.

———*I Never Had It Made: An Autobiography of Jackie Robinson.* As told to Alfred Duckett. New York: Putnam, 1972.

Robinson, Rachel. *Jackie Robinson: An Intimate Portrait.* With Lee Daniels. New York: Abrams, 2014.

Rowan, Carl T. *Wait Till Next Year: The Story of Jackie Robinson.* With Jackie Robinson. New York: Random House, 1960.

Smith, Claire. "A Grand Tribute to Robinson and His Moment." *New York Times,* April 16, 1997.

Tygiel, Jules. *Baseball's Great Experiment: Jackie Robinson and His Legacy.* New York: Oxford University Press, 1983.

IF YOU WANT TO LEARN MORE ABOUT JACKIE ROBINSON

Books

DeAngelis, Gina. *Jackie Robinson.* Philadelphia: Chelsea House, 2000.

Herman, Gail. *Who Was Jackie Robinson?* Illustrated by John O'Brien. New York: Grosset & Dunlap, 2011.

Robinson, Sharon. *Promises to Keep: How Jackie Robinson Changed America.* New York: Scholastic, 2004.

———. *Stealing Home: An Intimate Family Portrait by the Daughter of Jackie Robinson.* New York: Harper, 1996.

———. *Testing the Ice: A True Story About Jackie Robinson.* Illustrated by Kadir Nelson. New York: Scholastic, 2009.

Websites

Baseball Almanac
www.baseball-almanac.com

Jackie Robinson: The Official Website
www.jackierobinson.com

The Jackie Robinson Foundation
www.jackierobinson.org

National Baseball Hall of Fame and Museum
http://baseballhall.org

INDEX